THROWN IN

READY OR NOT, YOU ARE THE LEADER

MARK BOWSER

MADE FOR
SUCCESS

Made for Success Publishing
P.O. Box 1775 Issaquah, WA 98027
www.MadeForSuccessPublishing.com

Distributed by Made for Success Publishing

First Printing

Library of Congress Cataloging-in-Publication data

Bowser,Mark

   THROWN IN: Ready or Not, You are the Leader

     p. cm.

LCCN: 2021946339

ISBN: 9781641466622 (Paperback)

ISBN: 9781641466615 (eBook)

Printed in the United States of America

For further information contact Made for Success Publishing
+14255266480 or email service@madeforsuccess.net

WHAT ARE PEOPLE SAYING ABOUT
THROWN IN?

"The best way to communicate is through storytelling. In his book *Thrown In*, Mark Bowser tells a very effective story on what leadership is and how you can achieve it. It is never too late to get better. This book will help you do just that."

—**Lee Cockerell** (Retired and Inspired), Executive Vice President, Walt Disney World® and Author of *Creating Magic: 10 Leadership Strategies from a Life at Disney, The Customer Rules, Time Management Magic* and *Career Magic*

"Mark Bowser has written a fantastic little book in *Thrown In*. Unlike many boring business books, Mark teaches the principles of successful leadership in the form of an inspirational story. Let the mysterious fictional mentor Digger Jones teach you how to become the leader that others want to follow. *Thrown In* gets my vote — Five Stars!!"

—**Chris Widener**, Author of *Above All Else, The Angel Inside* and *Twelve Pillars with Jim Rohn*

"Great leadership has always been about moral influence. I have experienced firsthand Mark's remarkable capacity for leadership for forty years. In *Thrown In*, he demonstrates his giftedness for storytelling by seamlessly weaving together timeless wisdom about the art and science of 'influence' with the help of world-class leadership masters including John Maxwell, John Wooden, Billy Graham, Abraham Lincoln, and so many more."

—**Darrin Gray**, Author, Speaker, Leadership Advisor, @AllProDadLeader

"*Thrown In* is a heartwarming book with teeth. Heartwarming because it is written in the old Og Mandino form of an inspirational story. Teeth because it gives you the principles to becoming a great leader. Whether you are a seasoned leader or just starting out, *Thrown In* can take you to the next level."

—**Pat Williams**, Co-Founder of Orlando Magic and Author of *Character Carved In Stone*

"This book gets at the heart of what true leadership is all about and every manager, new or old, should have it on his or her desk."

—**Mike Kelly**, Founder, Right Path Enterprises

"In his book *Thrown In*, Mark has captured creative, thought-provoking, and time-tested principles that are memorable and applicable. They're presented in simple, innovative ways that will inspire you to become a more dynamic, influential leader."

—**Jeff Greer**, Senior Pastor, Grace Chapel, Mason, OH

"In Mark Bowser's *Thrown In*, he artfully tells a story that highlights what it takes to be a good and effective leader. Whether it is through learning about Disney's successes, through exploring seal training, or the power of storytelling, Bowser creatively paints a picture of the power that comes from the curiosity to read and explore the value provided by some of the top minds of our time. Use this as a roadmap to learn the importance of integrity, credibility, and influence to develop your *Thrown In*."

—**Dr. Diane Hamilton**, Ph.D., CEO of Tonerra, Author of *Cracking the Curiosity Code*

"Story is the most powerful teaching element in human learning, and Bowser capitalizes on this single truth. Combining history's greatest leaders, folktales, and theories, *Thrown In* is for every new leader wondering where to begin, and every seasoned leader dreaming of the next level."

—**Bryan Elsesser**, Sr. Dir. Sales Development, Leader, Coach, and Strategist at Aircall

"In a fast-changing world, many are unexpectedly called to leadership roles. Mark has made universal principles of effective leadership accessible by organizing them around a personal journey. This is a book that an emerging leader can read and put into practice immediately."

—**Adrian Davis**, President, Whetstone Inc.

CONTENTS

INTRODUCTION

ANDREW STEELE PLOPPED down in his desk chair in his second-floor office. The black leather creaked under the assault. "I hate this job," he muttered to no one but himself. "I just am not cut out for it." He looked up and saw the 16-by-20-inch painting of himself and his Uncle Steve given to him by the staff. He noticed the smiles on their faces in the painting and wondered why it had all so suddenly gone so wrong.

One afternoon, Uncle Steve had suffered a massive heart attack while sitting at his desk just down the hall from where Andrew sat now, and now he was gone. That was six months ago, and Andrew had inherited Steele Books from his uncle. Now, it was his job to run the company, and he wasn't doing so well at it. His uncle had always had this place humming like a well-oiled machine. Now, Andrew could barely hold on to his workers.

When Andrew's uncle had died, Steele Books had 86 employees and was the number two publisher of children's books in the United States and right on the heels of number one. Today, it was a different story. They were barely hanging on to the third position, and in the time since he had taken the reins, eight employees had quit, the latest being Fred Barnett—with whom Andrew had just lost his cool and instigated a shouting match in front of most of the staff.

What was he doing? He was much happier as a sales professional for the company. But Uncle Steve had had no children and had left the business to Andrew. Before his uncle's death, Andrew was liked and thought well of at the company. Now, the opposite was true. Or at least he thought so.

Andrew grabbed his jacket and headed for the door. "Suzy, I am gone for the day. I need to do some thinking," Andrew said to his secretary as he headed down the stairs two at a time and out the front door.

He pulled onto Meridian Avenue and headed towards downtown Indianapolis. He had lived in this city all his life. He knew where he needed to go. A place that always seemed to clear his mind.

Andrew parked his car and walked down the block to Monument Circle. Outside of the Colts stadium, it was probably the most famous place in the city. Andrew walked up the stairs, gazing up at the majestic figure on the top of the monument. He found a sturdy railing to lean on. He let the full weight of his upper body rest as he ran his fingers through his hair. "What am I going to do?" he said softly to himself.

"You are going to survive—and then you are going to flourish," said a gravelly, baritone voice behind him. Andrew's body jerked with surprise. He turned around to see an older man smiling at him. The older man wore a tailored, navy-blue-and-white-striped golf shirt and a pair of khaki walking shorts. He had the bluest eyes Andrew had ever seen and silver hair that was perfectly combed into place.

"Excuse me?" stammered Andrew.

"I said you are going to survive, and then you are going to flourish. I thought about saying 'thrive' instead of 'flourish,' but I thought that was a little corny," said the old man, chuckling to himself. "Let me introduce myself. My name is Digger Jones, and I have come to help you, Andrew Steele."

"What do you mean, you have come to help me?" asked Andrew defensively. "And... how do you know my name?"

"I know quite a bit about your situation. But that isn't important right now. Just know that I am a friend."

Somehow, he didn't know why, but Andrew trusted this strange older man who was offering him help. What kind of help, Andrew didn't know. And would it help? Only time would tell.

"Do you know the old diner over by the state fairgrounds on 38th Street?" asked Digger.

"The Tee Pee?"

"That's the one. Best hamburgers in town. Meet me there tomorrow at noon, and I will tell you how I can help you with your situation. Lunch is on me." With that, Digger smiled, gently turned away, and began walking down the limestone steps. He was about halfway down when he paused, turned, and said loudly, "I will see you tomorrow, Andrew."

About 45 minutes later, Andrew pulled his car into his driveway and up into the garage. He sat there for a moment thinking about this strange man named Digger Jones. For some reason, Andrew was feeling more hopeful than he had felt in months. He was actually looking forward to his lunch appointment tomorrow.

As Andrew entered the house through the garage, he walked directly into the warm light of his kitchen. There was his beautiful wife of eight years working on dinner at the island in the middle of the kitchen. In the background, he could hear their 5–year-old son Mike and 3-year-old daughter Carrie playing in the family room.

"Hi, honey," said Laura Steele with a smile. Her shoulder-length, reddish-brown hair framed her warm smile and deep brown eyes. "How was your day?"

"Hi, Sweetie. I had a… strange day."

"You OK?" said Laura with concern coming to her eyes.

"Sure. In fact, I am really good. I want to tell you all about it after we get the kids to bed."

Later that night, Andrew shared with Laura all about his very odd day. "Are you sure it is safe?" asked Laura. "I mean, meeting with this guy?"

"Yes, I think so. What harm could come of it?" A small smile creased the corners of his mouth. "I might even get a free lunch out of it."

The next day at 11:56 a.m., Andrew pulled into the parking lot of the Tee Pee Restaurant. From the parking lot, he could see the coliseum on the state fairgrounds. The old diner had been an Indianapolis fixture for over 50 years with its signature teepee sitting on top of the building, its own monument to the sky.

As Andrew walked in the front door, he saw an excited Digger Jones waving him to a booth. Sitting beside Digger was a slender, athletic man about the same age as Andrew.

Andrew walked over to the booth. "Good day to you," said an energetic Digger. "I am glad you could make it. Andrew, I hope you don't mind, but I also invited a good friend of mine to join us for lunch. This is Jack Blake."

After Andrew and Jack shook hands and exchanged the usual greetings, Digger said, "Jack here is one of my finest students of the past. He and I had our initial meeting at the old Cincinnati Zoo on a bench outside the gorilla enclosure. What is that big one's name?"

"Good ole Sam," said Jack. "He is incredible. Strong, courageous, confident. I get inspiration from him every time I see him."

All the things that I am not, Andrew thought.

"If you are like me, Andrew," continued Jack, "all the things you wish you were. But, let me tell you, without a doubt, you can be strong, courageous, and confident. And this is the man who can get you there." Jack pointed to Digger sitting right next to him in the booth.

"I was a struggling salesperson when Digger came to me on that bench those many years ago at the Cincinnati Zoo. He turned my business life around and taught me how to succeed. To toot my own horn just a little—to show you why you need to listen to this man—I have won many sales awards, and today I am the National Sales Director for my company."

"Not to mention one of the top motivational business speakers on the circuit today," cut in Digger. "Today, Jack is one of the most respected leaders in his industry."

"Thank you, Digger," said Jack. "But a good bit of the credit goes to you. You taught me and shaped me into a champion. And he can do the same for you, Andrew."

After a great lunch of burgers, fries, and chocolate milkshakes, Andrew was ready to get to the business of becoming a champion. He was sold on this Digger Jones and knew he was the man who could help him become the leader he needed to become.

"I asked Jack to bring along one of his audio programs. You see, not only is Jack's company one of the top sellers of audio, DVD, and digital motivational training programs, but his own program, *The Evolution of a Great Leader*, which is based on his best-selling book by the same title, has become the company's most popular leadership program. We are going to use it as the basis of our study together. And, from time to time, we are going to experience some other great leaders along the way." With that, Digger handed Andrew an iPod Touch. "We have taken the liberty of downloading Jack's *The Evolution of a Great Leader* for you. The iPod and the audio program are on me."

"Thank you very much. That is very generous," said Andrew, shocked at this man's kindness.

After a few more minutes of conversation, the three men stood up, shook hands, and went their separate ways. As Andrew watched Digger and Jack drive off in Digger's sporty convertible, Digger waved and said, "I will be in touch. Enjoy the first part of *The Evolution of a Great Leader.*"

As Andrew got into his car, he could hardly wait to start the audio program. He connected the iPod to his car stereo, pulled up the program, and pushed the arrow play key.

CHAPTER 1: WHAT IS LEADERSHIP, ANYWAY

AS ANDREW WAS pulling out of the Tee Pee Restaurant parking lot, the intro music played through his car stereo speakers. Then, an announcer began introducing Jack.

"Good evening, ladies and gentlemen. What is the one thing you can do that can propel you to success more than anything else? What is it that took a fledgling 13 colonies and transformed them into the greatest force for good on the face of the earth? Or the force that pulled back together the nation during the Civil War? What is it that shaped the great American companies of the past and is shaping the start-ups of tomorrow?

"That one thing, ladies and gentlemen, is leadership. Nothing more, nothing less. Becoming a good leader is the most important and the greatest investment you could ever make.

"Well, today, it is my great pleasure to introduce to you a man who can take that investment and make it into reality. That is, if you choose to take action on what you will learn tonight."

"The man I speak about is the author of the number one best-selling book, *The Evolution of a Great Leader*. Please welcome Jack Blake."

Andrew's excitement began to bubble up within him. He hadn't felt this hopeful in a long time—well, since his uncle passed away. Jack's baritone voice came through the car stereo speakers, and he began to speak.

● ● ● ●

What is leadership? We hear the term all the time. We talk about her being a good leader. We talk about him being a lousy leader. We talk about historical leaders, Fortune 500 leaders, church leaders, and even family leaders. But what is it?

In a nutshell, leadership is one word: INFLUENCE. Nothing more, nothing less. That is how J. Oswald Sanders defined it in his book many, many years ago. That is the best and most complete definition I have ever heard.

So, a leader influences the people around him. He influences them with his ideas, his vision, and even on what actions to take. What comes to your mind when I say the name "Hitler"? Was he a good leader? Take a look at our definition again. He definitely was influential. So, by our definition, he was an effective leader. But a good leader is something different.

Today, in *The Evolution of a Great Leader* seminar, we are going to talk about what it takes to be a good and effective leader. Hitler was effective, but he was far from good. So, let's get started.

Good and effective leaders are the greatest asset to any organization. With leaders like these, you can reach the stars. Without them, the murkiest swamp will become your home. As leadership expert John Maxwell said, "Everything rises and falls on leadership." Everything! Absolutely everything!

I believe that we have a true leadership gap in America today. I was talking with a friend of mine the other day who works in a big school district in Illinois. You would be amazed at what he said about his leaders. Then again, maybe you wouldn't be surprised. The things he told me they were doing or not doing break the rules of Leadership 101. I mean, they are basic. I don't know what they are teaching these education leaders at Administration School, but it certainly isn't leadership.

You see, leadership is both a science and an art. You have to understand both of the nuances, or you will fail as a leader. In his fabulous book, *Lincoln on Leadership*, Donald T. Phillips asks a very pointed question: "Why are there so few leaders in today's business community?" The answer seems to be that most managers simply don't understand or know enough about the nuts and bolts of skilled leadership. It's a difficult subject to master because there are no specifics that can be taught. And it is even more arduous to implement because doing so often involves trial and failure, pain and discomfort." So, together we are going to explore the science of leadership and give as many examples as we can of the art of leadership in action.

One of the first elements I believe we must understand is that there is a difference between an Influential Leader and a Positional Leader. The Positional Leader has the title. I am the President. I am the Director. I am the King of the company. Well, that is great. But the title doesn't in and of itself make a person influential. The Influential Leader may be the peasant of the kingdom or the entry-level employee. Influence is about inspiring and moving people into action in order to reach a desired goal. I hope you have the position within your company, but I also hope you have the trust, respect, and heart of your people.

How does a one-time traveling salesman who had once studied law impact the whole world? Through influence. You may not know his name, but I am confident you know of his impact. You may have felt it yourself. His name was Mordecai Ham. Doesn't ring a bell? How about this name—Billy Graham? Oh, you have heard of him, huh! Well, these two are eternally linked.

After Mordecai Ham had been ordained into the ministry, he became a fairly well-known minister in his denomination but achieved his real impact on the world when he was asked to hold a series of meetings in Charlotte, North Carolina.

Dr. Ham was a very controversial figure who elicited many an opinion about him wherever he went. One such opinion was from a teenage Billy Graham. Graham said in his autobiography, "Despite my parents' enthusiasm, I did not want anything to do with anyone called an evangelist—and particularly with such a colorful character as Dr. Ham. Just turning sixteen, I told my parents that I would not go to hear him."

Well, a few weeks went by. Ham was still preaching in Charlotte, and Billy was still holding true to his word. He still hadn't heard Ham speak. Then everything began to change. Ham had proclaimed that there was some immoral behavior linked to Central High School. Some of the students had gotten very upset about Ham's accusation, and it was rumored they were going to protest in front of where he was preaching. There was even talk that the students might do some bodily harm to the preacher.

This sparked the curiosity of young Billy. Not that he wanted to participate; he just wanted to see what would happen. But how could he save face? He had told his parents he would not go hear Ham speak. And he had held out for weeks. That is when another influential leader entered the story. His name was Albert McMakin.

Albert egged Billy on: "Why don't you come out and hear our fighting preacher?"

"A fighter? That is cool," thought Billy. Well, Billy decided to go with his friend Albert and as many people as they could fit into Albert's old vegetable truck. Something happened that night. Billy was transfixed by the words of this fiery troublemaker who stood on the platform.

From that night on, Billy sat there listening to Ham every single night—for weeks. One night, he responded by walking to the front of the platform when Ham gave the invitation to become a Christian. Billy was one of over 300 people who went forward that night.

That is when yet another influential leader made his impact. He was a family friend of the Grahams, and his name was J.D. Prevatt. He was a local tailor. When J.D.

saw Billy standing at the platform that night, he walked up to him and put his arm around him. He explained the Gospel to Billy in everyday language so that he could better understand it. Then he encouraged young Billy to give his life to Jesus Christ and told him how to do that. Billy made that commitment and later became one of the greatest evangelists in history.

Think back at that story for a moment. Without the influence of these three fairly unknown leaders, Billy Graham may have turned out very differently. And, if that would have happened, think about the millions around the world who would not have experienced his life-changing impact on their lives. Great change and great impact are made by influential leaders.

Influential leaders come in all shapes, sizes, and ages. It is the power of their ideas and how they can express those ideas that make the difference.

Imagine yourself in a small, quaint local café in England. You can smell the aroma of the coffee as it brews in the pot just a few feet from your booth. Your napkin moves ever so slightly beside your plate from the breeze as a waitress hustles by to serve another table. As you look around, you see a number of businesspeople chatting quietly, but there at a corner table, you see something different. It is a lady around 30, maybe 35 years old, writing something on some scrap paper. She writes feverishly as if she has to get the thoughts down before they whisk away. Who is this lady? What is she writing? It must be important—at least to her.

What you just witnessed is very similar to what happened in another English café as a struggling single mother wrote down the beginnings of a story that would change the literary world and the culture forever. J.K. Rowling is an influential leader like none other in the literary world. Her Harry Potter series of books has not only entertained millions of people, but literally changed the economy of many industries like books, movies, and games. Not to mention the resulting cultural references that have become a part of the fabric of our time. That is leadership, and she has accomplished it simply through the power of her ideas.

There is another writer, at another time, who we could say had an even bigger impact. In fact, I can say that without this man and his words, America may not be a country today. So, who is this master influencer of American history? Was it Washington, Jefferson, Franklin? No, but they all knew him… or at least knew of him. I am talking about Thomas Paine. His pamphlet Common Sense convinced a nation that tyranny must be stopped and that independence must be sought. General Washington was known to pass out copies of some of Paine's writings to the troops to inspire them before a battle.

Influence or Position: which is more important? It is always influence. You can have the highest position in the land but no power to sway action. You can only have influence at your disposal—and the power to change an entire world.

Before we can go any further, I believe it is important that we dig a little deeper into the explanations and actions of leadership. Let me ask you a question. Is there a difference between a leader and a manager? There is a big difference, isn't there! The late Dr. Stephen R. Covey used to say, "Leaders lead people, and managers lead things." Hmmm, interesting… and so true.

So, when we think about action steps, what exactly does a leader do? What is the first action that they take? They create the direction of the organization or team. They create a vision. They may not create a vision for the entire organization, but they definitely do for their department.

If the leader creates the vision, then what does the manager do? They make it happen. They implement the vision. The leader creates where we are going, and the manager breaks the vision into manageable parts, assigns the tasks to the right people, and assures that they accomplish those tasks.

Another term we hear quite often is "coach." Where does a coach fall into this equation? A coach motivates, inspires, teaches, provides resources, and disciplines when necessary.

In a nutshell, which are we? Are we a leader, a manager, or a coach? I believe that we are all three. I don't think we can separate it anymore. To be the most effective that we can be at influencing those around us, we have to be a leader, a manager, and a coach. For the sake of ease, in most cases in this program, I am going to use the terms "Leader" and "Leadership," but I am talking about all three ideas rolled into one.

• • • •

Andrew pulled into his parking spot at Steele Books and turned off the car and iPod. "This is incredible," he thought. "I am going to turn this business around. I am going to become the leader that God has created me to be. I am going to do it. I know I will!"

Before getting out of the car, he excitedly pulled his iPhone from his pocket and quickly dialed his wife.

"Hi, Honey," came the sweet sound of Laura's voice. "How was your lunch meeting?"

"Absolutely incredible," said Andrew. "Digger gave me an iPod Touch with an awesome program on it titled *The Evolution of a Great Leader*, which is a live seminar based on the number one best-selling book by Jack Blake. And guess what, Sweetie?"

"What? It is great to hear enthusiasm in your voice again!"

"I met him."

"Who?" asked a bewildered Laura.

"Jack Blake. I just had lunch with Jack Blake. He is a former student of Digger's."

"Are you serious? Are you pulling my leg?"

"Laura, I am absolutely serious. Digger is going to use Jack's program as a resource in mentoring me. I feel like I am in a dream."

"Wow! That is incredible. So, this Digger Jones guy is the real deal."

"He certainly is, Sweetie. I can't wait to tell you all about it when I get home tonight. I am back at work now. I am still in the car. I can't wait to get back in the office. See you tonight. I love you, Laura."

"I love you, too, Honey. See you tonight."

CHAPTER 2: GETTING OTHERS TO BUY INTO YOUR IDEAS

"**Y**OU HAVE TO put something in before you can get something out. You have to invest and connect with your people before you can expect them to trust and follow you," said Digger in his trademark gravelly baritone voice to Andrew as they walked on the cool grass at Mounds State Park in Anderson, Indiana.

Digger had convinced Andrew that morning to drive the 40-some miles northeast of Indianapolis to clear his mind with new surroundings. Digger had specifically chosen Mounds. Its historic value and serene scenery made it the perfect place for him to inspire his young protégé.

Digger and Andrew walked in silence. The only sound was the central Indiana breeze rustling through the leaves of the sycamore trees. Not far off, a plump brown squirrel scuttled up a nearby tree with its treasure in its mouth. Every so often, Digger would glance over at Andrew to see if any of this was getting through to him.

Andrew had been particularly melancholy the last couple of days. Digger had reminded him that success takes time. Andrew had hoped that his people would have responded quicker to his new leadership skills.

The two men walked up to a large area of the park where an old-fashioned brown picket fence surrounded a large circular earthwork. As Andrew leaned up against the fence with his left hand, he ran his right over the rough edge of the fence. He could feel each groove of the wood. He thought how easy it would be to get a splinter. At that moment, Andrew jerked his hand back as he felt the sting of a needle-thin piece of wood that had just sliced into his index finger. "Great. Just great," he thought.

Digger didn't even seem to notice. "Andrew, what you see before you is the Great Mound. It was thought to have been built around 160 B.C. by the Adena-Hopewell Native Americans, most likely for ceremonial or community gatherings.

"Think about this masterpiece. These people had no modern Bobcat earthmovers or digging equipment. They had to dig this with their bare hands or, at the very least, the most basic of shovels. This place is a metaphor for what you are experiencing right now.

"The Adena-Hopewell people had to invest for this place to exist today," Digger continued. "It didn't happen overnight. By the sweat of their brow, it is here for us to enjoy today. Not just by sweat but also through community. They couldn't do it by themselves. They had to work together. The same is true with you, my young friend. These historic people struggled together through the challenges, the ups and downs, and who knows how long and how many hardships to build something worthy—together. And here it is. Right here in front of us."

Digger paused and then quietly said, "Listen to me, Andrew. You have what it takes. You are becoming an extraordinary leader, but you and your team are experiencing the baggage of the past. The baggage will be overwhelmed by the present. It just takes time. The seeds you have planted are growing. They are just under the surface.

"The farmer doesn't see any growth in the late spring. But he knows the growth is there. He has faith in the seeds he has planted and that by mid-summer, he will begin to see the fruit of his continued labors."

"I know you are right," said Andrew as he now slid his left hand over the wood fence. He then remembered the splinter on his right hand and simply dropped his left arm to his side. As he did, he felt the warm, strong weight of Digger's hand on his shoulder. "I am just a little down right now."

"I know you are. Let's take a walk down by the river," said Digger as he steered Andrew toward the river trail.

Around 2:30 in the afternoon, Andrew and Digger pulled into the parking lot of Steele Books. Andrew thanked his mentor and then watched as Digger drove off in that pale blue 1982 classic convertible Cadillac. Digger gave an exuberant wave as he drove off. Andrew weakly waved back. He was better after their talk and journey to the earthworks of the Adena-Hopewell people, but he was still down.

Andrew walked in the door of his office building and could hear Jacob Smithson, one of his editors, talking with someone. Instead of going up the stairs to his own office, Andrew turned down the hallway towards Jacob's office. "Time to plant more seeds," Andrew thought.

He paused about five and a half feet from the entrance to Jacob's open office door. He wanted to be a servant leader for his people. He cared about them and wanted to see them succeed. After a moment's reflection, Andrew popped his head in the door.

"What are you boys working on?" asked Andrew as he leaned up against the far side of the white-finished door frame.

"Oh. Hi, Andrew," said Jacob. "We are having a little challenge with the format of a book."

Andrew walked into the office and extended his hand to the other man who was sitting next to Jacob at the round conference table in the small office. "Hi. My name is Andrew Steele."

"I'm R.H. Dunlap."

"Andrew," broke in Jacob. "R.H. is the author of a new adventure book series for 12 to 16-year-olds."

"It is an honor to meet you, R.H. We are glad to have you on board with us." Andrew made a gesture toward the one remaining empty chair at the table. Looking at Jacob, he said, "May I?"

"Of course," said Jacob, a bit shocked at this gesture from his boss.

"You boys mentioned that you were having a little trouble with the format of your books. Maybe I can help," said Andrew.

"That would be wonderful," said R.H. He and Jacob then went on to explain the challenges they were having weaving the story together. Andrew sat quietly, absorbing every word. This went on for 20, maybe 30 minutes. As Andrew asked insightful questions, his enthusiasm for the work began to show forth. This is what had made Andrew such a successful sales professional in the past. He was always so passionate about books, particularly books for kids. Andrew was beginning to realize that he was still selling. As a leader, he had to sell himself, his ideas, and his vision.

"R.H., you have a great concept, and it sounds like you have already done some great work on the series," said Andrew. "What might help is if we storyboard it."

"Storyboard it?" asked Jacob. "I mean, I have heard of the concept but have never thought of using it for a book or series."

"I think it may help," continued Andrew. "Storyboarding is a concept made famous by Disney. One of Walt's animators liked to spread everything on the floor so he could look down on it and see the whole picture. Imagine a whole slew of pencil sketches of an animated short or movie spread out over the entire carpet." Andrew made a sweeping, gesturing motion toward the floor of Jacob's office. It was as if he could see the animated pictures all over the floor. His belief was so strong that Jacob and R.H. began to see the pictures as well.

"When Walt would walk into the office of this animator, he would see a menagerie of papers on the floor. He hated it. So he asked the animator to clean it up. The next time Walt walked into the office, it was all cleaned up. Only now, all the pictures had been pinned up on the wall. Walt didn't like that either. He complained now that the animator had put a bunch of pinholes in his wall."

"The next time Walt walked into the office, he loved what he saw. The animator had taken down all the pinned pictures and placed them on a large piece of wood, which he then hung on the wall. Walt could see the entire feature or short in a sequence of scenes or pictures. He then implemented the idea of storyboarding studio-wide.

"Storyboarding," continued Andrew, "gives a sense of continuity or sequence to make a story flow better. Or it helps show when the story *isn't* flowing. Let's take your ideas and storyboard them out."

Andrew, Jacob, and R.H. then went on to outline his entire book series like Walt and his animators did for a major animation movie. The only difference was that instead of pictures, Andrew, Jacob, and R.H. wrote a brief description of what was happening in each scene.

"This is great," said R.H. with a smile as he looked over his entire series spread out in front of him.

"Thanks for your help, Andrew," said Jacob. "We couldn't have done this without you."

"I was glad to help. You guys did most of the work. I just shared an organizational concept." At that moment,

Andrew's cell phone rang. He looked down at his iPhone and saw that it was his wife who was calling. Andrew picked it up and said, "Hi, Sweetie."

"You all right?" asked Laura Steele.

"Sure. Why do you ask?"

"Because it is so late. You are usually home by now."

Andrew twisted his wrist and looked at his watch. It was 6:23 p.m. "I am sorry, Sweetie. I had no idea it was this late. Jacob and one of our brand-new authors, R.H. Dunlap, were working on his book series. R.H. has written a masterpiece. I will be home in just a few minutes." R.H. beamed as he heard Andrew compliment his books.

As Andrew was finishing up his phone call with Laura, he started for the door. After he and Laura said their good-byes, he placed his iPhone back into its belt holster. As he did, he said to Jacob and R.H., "Great work today. I gotta run. I am late for family dinner. My wife was worried. She takes good care of me. Great to see you, R.H. Say 'Hi' to Sylvia for me, Jacob."

With that, Andrew walked out of Jacob's office and headed for the outside door and his car.

A couple of days later, Andrew and Digger were teeing off on the fourth hole of the Indy Valley Golf Course. It was a beautiful day, sunny with a few clouds and 83 degrees. But for Andrew, what made it such a beautiful day was his team was beginning to respond. For the first three holes, Andrew had been telling Digger about his afternoon with Jacob and author R.H. Dunlap.

The course only had a few golfers on it that day, which made it a perfect place for Digger and Andrew to talk, walk, and play at their own pace. With his signature gravelly voice and enthusiasm, Digger said, "What you are experiencing is the fruits of 'The Law of Buy-In.'"

"The Law of Buy-In?" asked Andrew.

"Yes. It is a John Maxwell term. John wrote about it in his fabulous book *The 21 Irrefutable Laws of Leadership*. You should read that book, Andrew. In this particular law, Maxwell points out that 'People buy into the leader then the vision.' I believe you made two disciples the other day in Jacob and R.H. What you did, Andrew, was sell yourself first by being willing to spend time with them and serve them in overcoming their challenge with R.H.'s book series. By the way, that was brilliant how you weaved in Disney's storyboarding. I have always been a fan of Walt Disney and the storyboarding organizational method.

"You showed Jacob and R.H. that you believed in them and their abilities to overcome the mental block they found themselves in. You also expressed to them your belief in the book series and the decisions they had already made. This is like a coach believing in a basketball player to take the last shot. It is huge!

"Andrew, you also helped them see a bright future of success for the book series. They caught that belief, and they bought into you. This process all began when you took the time to serve them. Today, we hear a lot about the term 'servant leadership,' but I think it sometimes gets lost in all the flowery metaphors. All it is is spending time with your people and finding ways to help them.

Maxwell also said that 'People don't care how much you know until they know how much you care.' You showed them you cared, and—to risk sounding flowery—you showed love for them, Andrew. That is the key to them buying into you."

With that, Digger teed off. It was a long drive just to the left of center of the fairway about 280 yards down. Perfect location for Digger to land on the green with his next shot.

CHAPTER 3: THE THREE FACTS OF LEADERSHIP

THE NEXT MORNING, Andrew arrived in his office at 7. The office was completely empty and as quiet as the vacuum of space. After talking with Digger, Andrew had decided to start a daily study time every workday before the others arrived. I should have about an hour, he thought.

He flipped on the light and walked over to the couch located against the far wall. He sat down, took the iPod Touch out of his pocket, and opened his planner to the notes section.

Jack Blake's familiar voice began.

• • • •

Before we get into the nuts and bolts of the elements of leadership, let's pause for a moment and talk about three fundamental facts of leadership. Understanding these three facts will help jumpstart your development as a more influential individual.

FACT #1: ONE PERSON CAN MAKE A DIFFERENCE

Most of us have heard that statement before. It is obviously not original with me. But what images came to your mind when you heard that statement? If you are like many people, an image of Billy Graham, Dr. Martin Luther King, Jr., or Mother Teresa came to mind. However, do you see someone missing from that list? I do. That someone is YOU!

Mother Teresa didn't go out to become a saint; she went out to save one dying person. She was walking down the street and saw someone dying in a gutter. She said to herself, "That is not right. Everyone should die with dignity." You see, great leaders look at the world differently. The great leaders strive to figure out how they can touch a life, and by taking that action, their influence may touch hundreds, thousands, and maybe even millions of lives.

So the question is, where can your leadership grow to make a bigger impact than it does today? You are probably already making a difference, but how can your leadership grow? You make a difference, and people need you!

FACT #2: YOU NEED TO START LEADING TODAY

Many times, young leaders will say, "I'm not ready to lead. I need to wait till I read that leadership book, or go to that management seminar, or learn that skill." Now, those are all important things, and I encourage them, but the truth of the matter is that your team can't wait. You need to start leading today—and to learn as you lead. None of us will ever know all there is to leadership. It is a continual growing process. We can't wait until we know all there is to leadership, or we will do absolutely nothing. We must take action every day to become influential and grow continually throughout our leadership journey.

FACT #3: THE OFFICE DOESN'T MAKE THE PERSON

Leadership is not about the corner office. Have you ever worked for someone who thought that was true? They were more concerned with their promotion, their prestige, and their accolades. In the process, they lost their team (and many times their customers) as a result.

Now, please don't misunderstand me; I have no problem with comfortable offices and a comfortable work environment. In fact, I am for it. Today, my office suite is very comfortable. But it wasn't always that way. I remember a dingy apartment when I was starting out as a struggling salesperson. My kitchen table, which was actually a folding card table, doubled as my desk. It wasn't until I met my mentor Digger Jones that things began to look up for me.

On a side note, you need to get a mentor. Everyone can benefit from a coach. A person who knows the path and can shine a light as you follow that path. Even Michael Jordan had a coach. Great actors have acting coaches. Musicians have teachers. We all can benefit from having a mentor.

Anyway, back to the topic at hand. We must never put the cart before the horse. Today, my office suite is very comfortable. We have luxuries today that I thought we would never have. But—and here is the kicker—we have ample resources today to have those luxuries.

Always be more concerned with helping your team succeed and serving your customers than about having the cushy sofa and picture window in your office. Those things will come. Create loyalty out of your team and your customers. Focus on your team and focus on your customers, and the rest will take care of itself.

● ● ● ●

"Good morning, Andrew." His receptionist Suzy awakened him from his focus. He turned off the iPod and pulled out his earbuds.

"Good morning Suzy. How are you this morning?"

"I am great. You are in early."

"Yes. I wanted to have some quiet study time to start my day."

"Oh, I am sorry to disturb you."

"Quite all right. I had lost track of time. What do you say we go create some incredible books today?"

With a smile, Suzy replied, "Sounds good to me, Sir."

CHAPTER 4: THE SERVANT LEADER

"**A**NDREW, AS I** have said before, the most effective and best leaders are those who are servants," said Digger as he bit into his cinnamon crunch bagel. "Servant leadership is not just a term that sounds good. It is a way of life."

Andrew and Digger had met for an early morning breakfast at Panera Bread. It was 6:15, and there were only a few early-riser patrons in the restaurant.

Digger bent his head just a bit and raised his hands over his mouth, almost in a praying fashion. He paused as if in deep thought and then said, "Tony Campolo used to tell a story that seems to be appropriate here. It is a true story. As you know, during World War II, the Nazis made an abominable habit of rounding up all the Jews for slaughter. Well, the Nazi S.S. troops made their way to a small Polish village and gathered up all the Jewish people they could find. Dads, moms, children, and neighbors were gathered in one place. They were then forced to dig the shallow graves that would be their own. With perspiration pouring from their bodies from exertion and nerves, they were forced to turn and face the firing squad. The bullets began to fly. Bodies riddled with machine-gun bullets fell backward into the shallow graves. One little boy witnessed the killing of his parents, but even though he was standing next to them, he was somehow spared a bullet. Splattered with his parents' blood, the little boy plunged himself onto their bodies in the grave and pretended to be dead himself.

"After the massacre, the Nazi troops filled in the graves with dirt. Since they were so shallow, air was able to filter down to the boy to keep him alive. Hours went by. Can you imagine what it must have been like lying on the bodies of your family—not to mention being buried alive?

"Well, when he felt it was safe, the little boy dug himself out of the grave. He ran to the nearest house and asked for help. But they turned him away. Why would anyone do that? They were afraid. They recognized him as one of the Jewish boys marked by the Nazis for death. They thought that if they helped him, then they would suffer the vengeance of the S.S. troops. This happened at house after house.

"Finally, as the little boy knocked on the door of yet another house, the occupants inside could hear him crying, 'Don't you recognize me? I am the Jesus you say you love.' A moment went by, and then a woman flung open the door, wrapped her arms around the little boy, and kissed him. From that day on, the little boy became a member of that family as if he had been born into it."

Digger looked up at Andrew with moistness in his eyes. Andrew had never seen this kind of emotion out of his crusty old mentor. Digger said, "Andrew, that is what leadership is all about. Many times, your team members need to know that their leader cares. Not just about the bottom line or the work at hand. But that they really care—about *them*."

CHAPTER 5: LEADERS ASK QUESTIONS

A COUPLE OF nights later, Digger joined Andrew and his family for dinner at the Steele home. "Thanks for inviting me, Mrs. Steele," said Digger.

"Oh, you are welcome, Mr. Jones. And please call me Laura. Andrew has said so much about you that I feel like I have known you for years like an uncle."

"I like that, Laura. You can call me Digger, or Uncle Digger if you prefer," said the old man with a sparkle in his eyes.

"Uncle Digger it is. Uncle Digger, I would like to introduce you to our children. This handsome young man is Mike, and he is 5 years old, and this beautiful little princess is Carrie, and she is 3 years old."

Digger leaned over and held out his hand to Mike. "How do you do, young sir?" And he shook Mike's hand. Digger then turned to Carrie and said, "It is my honor, young miss," as he shook her hand, too.

Digger then looked at both of them. "Let me ask the two of you a question, and here it is. Did you ask a good question today?"

The two Steele children looked at him with puzzlement on their faces. Their parents wore the same puzzled face. "No, I am serious," said Digger to all of them. "Did you ask a good question today? I tell you what, when we sit down to eat, I will tell you a little story."

After a few minutes, Laura called them all to the table. "Mike, did you wash your hands?" A sheepish frown came over the little boy's face as he looked at his mother. "Well, you know what to do," said Laura. "Make it quick. We are waiting for you."

After Andrew led them in saying grace, he looked at Digger. "All right, Dig, I can hardly wait to hear your story."

"What story is that, Andrew?" asked Digger.

"You know, the one about asking questions."

"Oh yeah. I almost forgot about that. Well, anyway, in 1944, Isidor Isaac Rabi was awarded the Nobel Prize for his work on atomic nuclei. He was a nuclear physicist.

"After his acceptance speech, he was asked about some of the key points of his life. In particular, what were the greatest influences that made the biggest difference for him? Isidor spoke about growing up in Brooklyn, New York, and one of the key moments of his life happened every night. He explained that most of his friends were asked by their parents what they had learned in school that day. But not his mom. She asked him a very different question. Every day when he arrived home from school, his mom would ask him, 'Izzy, did you ask a good question today?' You see, that is a very different question," said Digger.

"Isidor said that question from his mom every day helped him develop a curiosity which birthed his academic success and, later on, his success in physics."

Looking right at Mike and Carrie, Digger said, "Kids, always remember that questions open the door to your success."

"Dig, that is a great story," said Andrew. "I can see how that is a great focus for leaders, too."

"Absolutely," said Digger. "Leaders get things accomplished not on an island by themselves but through people. Learning and making it a habit to ask yourself and your team questions is a huge key to influence and creative breakthroughs. No solution is revealed until the question is asked."

"What kind of questions should a leader ask themselves?" asked Laura.

"That is a very good question in and of itself," Digger teased. But, seriously, here are some of the most important questions that, in my opinion, a leader can ask themselves on a consistent basis:

What did I learn today?

What difference did I make today?

What questions did I ask today?

What did I improve today?

What are my goals today?

What is the most important thing for me to work on today?

What is my plan for tomorrow?

"And that is just a sampling of the most important questions."

"Excuse me," said Andrew as he stood up.

"Where are you going, Honey?" asked Laura.

"I will only be a minute. I want to write these thoughts and questions down so I don't forget them."

"Good man," said Digger.

CHAPTER 6: A MADE BED, A MADE LIFE

"**W**HAT ARE YOU working on, Honey?" asked Laura as she walked into the family room with a laundry basket.

"Well, I am working on my presentation for tomorrow," said Andrew.

"Is tomorrow the day of your first whole team meeting? What are you calling them again?"

"Yeah. It is tomorrow morning at 9. I am calling them our Weekly Motivational Summit. I am looking forward to it, except I am having a little trouble knowing what to talk about tomorrow. Oh, let me help you with the laundry."

"No, I got it. Thanks though. What do you have so far for the meeting?"

Andrew turned around his iPad and showed her the screen. "I have the outline done, including my vision for the future of Steele Books. At the end of every meeting, I have a place for about a 15-minute motivational moment or speech. I am just not sure what to put in there."

"How about talking about something that inspires you? Yesterday you were pretty excited as you told me about a book you had just finished—a book by some Admiral."

"Oh, yeah. Great idea, Laura. That is *Make Your Bed*, by Admiral William McRaven. That book has an awesome message. It would make a great message to share with my team. Thanks, Sweetie."

With a smile, Laura said, "That is what I am here for." By this time, she had all the laundry folded. "I will leave you to it. I am going to put the laundry up and check on the kids, too. They should be sound asleep by now."

WEEKLY MOTIVATIONAL SUMMIT

The next morning, Andrew was the first one in the small auditorium that his uncle had insisted on adding to the design of the building before they built it. His uncle Steve had never mentioned his plans for this 300-seat auditorium, and he didn't live long enough to put those mysterious plans into motion.

At the front of the auditorium was a stage that spanned the entire width of the auditorium. The room itself was a half-circle with seats arcing around the stage. Andrew always thought it would make a great venue for a dramatic play or musical. The seats sported crimson fabric, and the floor had a slight incline in it to ensure a great view for all attendees.

Andrew felt good about his future plans for this space, and he was excited about sharing it with his team—as well as his plans for the future of Steele Books. Right at 9 o'clock, Andrew's troops began to assemble through the two sets of double doors at the rear of the auditorium.

After giving them two or three minutes to get settled, Andrew walked to the center of the stage. He wore a wireless microphone with a boom that wrapped around his right cheek in front of his mouth. Andrew began to speak:

"Good morning! Welcome to our first Weekly Motivational Summit. Right here at the beginning, let me ask you a question—let me ask us *all* a question. If you could accomplish anything, and everything was a possibility, then where would you be in 12 months?

"You see, the GPS that is a part of the phone in your pocket is worthless if you don't input a destination. Sure, the GPS knows where you are. It knows the starting position because it can calculate that. But only you can calculate the destination. And destination is always a choice.

"Our Weekly Motivational Summit meetings are designed to help you reach your destination. Did you notice I said your destination and not the destination of Steele Books? I believe that if I give it my all to help you reach your greatest desires, the dreams of your heart, then the ship of Steele Books is secure and will reach all its safe harbors. And why can I say that? Because you are the motor of the ship. Without you, the ship would never leave the dock. With you, the ship can travel the world's seas and reach any destination.

"So, you might be thinking, 'Andrew, then what is your job on the ship? Are you the rudder?' Well, in a way. I do set some direction, and we are going to talk about the vision of Steele Books this morning. But, more importantly, I see myself as your coach and your cheerleader.

"Many years ago, Walt Disney was giving a group of children a tour of his studio. One child asked, 'Mr. Disney, do you draw the cartoons and movies?' Walt had to admit that he didn't do that anymore. Questions like that continued. 'Mr. Disney, do you do this? Mr. Disney, do you do that?' For each question, Walt had to admit that he didn't do those things. One child finally looked up into the eyes of the entertainment genius and asked, 'Mr. Disney, then what is it that you *do*?'

"Walt thought about that for a moment and then answered the question something like this: 'Well, I am kind of like a little bee. I fly from office to office, and I kind of pollinate things. That is my job.'"

Andrew paused and looked up as if seeing into Heaven and said, "Well said, Mr. Disney. Well said.

"So, this morning, I want to share my vision for Steele Books and where our destination lies, and then I am going to give you a little pollination that, if acted upon, will help you reach your dreams. Sound good? Well then, let's get started.

"First of all, the future of this auditorium. You have probably wondered why we have this space and what we are going to use it for. I have been wondering the same thing myself. This auditorium was a dream of my uncle's. He never really shared what his vision was for it. All I can say is that he would want it used to bring hope and joy to the team of Steele Books and the wider community.

"With that spirit, we are renaming this room where we gather today the Steve Steele Auditorium: A Place Where Dreams Begin." With that, Vice President of Sales Chuck Harrison and Chief Operating Officer Sally Benjamin pushed a wheeled cart to the front of the stage. On the cart was a statue of Steve Steele that was about six feet high.

Andrew walked over to the lifelike statue of his uncle and said into the microphone, "Uncle Steve, this is for you. We will make you proud, and I know that we already have." He then turned to his team and continued, "You see how his hand is pointing forward? To some distant destination? That is us. Always stretching forward, always striving to improve, always seeking growth, always finding new, better ways to serve.

"This statue of Steve Steele will be placed at the entrance of this auditorium so that everyone who enters may know our proud heritage.

"So, how are we going to use this auditorium? Every Wednesday morning, we will have our Weekly Motivational Summit where we will share our vision and other important company information. During each meeting, you will also be presented a message of hope. Sometimes, like today, it will be delivered by me. Other times, other Steele Books leaders will share with us. Sometimes we might bring in a guest speaker. We would also like to offer you an opportunity to share a message. If you would be interested in this, then please drop a note or email to Suzy in my office.

"Another way we will use this space is that one Saturday night a month, we are going to have a movie night. All the movies will be family-friendly. So, bring your kids. Bring your friends. And bring your neighbors.

"Starting in two weeks from this Sunday, Nazarene Christian Church will be holding their services here. We are charging them no rent. It is a way we can give back. We hope to offer this space for other community events going forward, too.

"Now, let's talk for just a minute about where we are heading. When I took over after my uncle's death, we were the number two children's book publisher in the United States. Because of some mistakes I had made and some challenges I was dealing with, we have slipped to number three. But no more. Let's make a decision right now that we will settle for nothing short of our best. And I believe we can be number one." Andrew was shocked by the response. His team rose to their feet and, with enthusiasm, roared their approval. After the applause had ended and everyone was back in their seats, Andrew continued, "We have a plan to meet that goal, and together we will meet it."

Andrew paused and looked out at his team. Raw emotion tugged at his spirit. The team clapped and cheered at seeing how touched their leader had become. Regaining his composure, Andrew said, "You are the best. God surely has blessed me with an incredible team. More importantly, God has blessed me with the permission to walk this journey with you.

"Now, let me give you some inspiration on living your dreams…"

A voice in the back of the auditorium yelled, "You already have, Andrew." The team cheered again.

"Thank you. I really appreciate that. As I was thinking about what I could share with you today, my wonderful wife Laura suggested I share with you something that has inspired me of late. It is a book titled *Make Your Bed*. Kind of a strange title, isn't it? It was written by retired Navy Admiral William H. McRaven and has a great message.

"Today, we have a copy of this book for each of you. You will find them on tables at the back of the auditorium. Please take one as you leave after our meeting. It is kind of funny. The idea of sharing this message with you today was a little last minute—and then I got inspired to have a book here for each of you." Andrew chuckled. "You should have seen me last night and then again this morning. I was calling bookstores scrounging up as many copies as I could find. It took four bookstores and five voice messages to find enough. And then, Chuck and I divided and conquered this morning and went to those bookstores to pick up the books. We even opened a couple of the stores, didn't we, Chuck?" Chuck nodded and smiled, and the crowd laughed.

"Anyway," continued Andrew, "we have books for you in the back. Please make sure you get a copy. You are going to love it.

"Admiral McRaven spent over 30 years on the Navy's elite SEAL Team. In 2014, he was asked to give the graduation commencement address at his alma mater, the University of Texas. That speech was such a success that the Admiral expanded on his message and turned it into the incredible book you will get today. I also encourage you to go to YouTube and listen to his entire 2014 speech.

"Admiral McRaven was having difficulty crafting a speech for the graduating seniors at UT. Much like my wife Laura, the Admiral's wife said, 'Why don't you share something you know.' Well, he had spent most of his life as a Navy SEAL. That is what he knew. So he put together a presentation of 10 points he learned from SEAL training. If acted upon, they can help anyone—whether they are in the military or the private sector—succeed in life.

"For the sake of time, I am only going to share with you seven of the Admiral's ten points. I also will add a few of my thoughts to these principles as we go along. So, let's get started.

"Number one, make your bed every day. Every morning during SEAL training, the instructors would inspect the trainees' beds. Your bed had to be perfectly made. On the surface, this seemed kind of a dumb exercise. After all, these guys were training to be some of the most elite warriors on the planet.

"But the Admiral said that this mundane exercise and its importance came back to him over and over as the years passed. You see, by making your bed every morning after you rise, you will have accomplished the first task of the day. It is your first success of many successes to come. One success gives you the confidence that you can reach another success and another and another and another. And, if by chance you happen to have an absolutely terrible day, the Admiral pointed out you at least will come home to a bed that is made. It is a success that you accomplished, and by so doing, no day will be a complete failure. So, in order to succeed in life, make your bed every day.

"Number two, in order to win, you need to have a team. During SEAL training, the trainees always had to carry a large rubber boat with them. Now, they didn't have to do it on their own. The boat team consisted of seven

SEAL trainees. When you went to the chow hall, you had your boat. When you went to the head, also known as the bathroom, you had your boat. Everywhere you went, you had to take your boat with you.

"When you were in your boat in the ocean, it took teamwork to paddle in the high surf in Southern California. If one side of trainees didn't pull their weight, the boat would capsize.

"When a member of the team wasn't feeling particularly perky on a given day—maybe they had the flu or a cold—were they allowed to stay in their bunk? No way! The team needed them, and they needed the team. On these days, you carried a little extra weight and pushed a little harder because your buddy needed you. You did this not only because it was right but also because you knew he would do it for you when you were in need.

"Nobody reaches the top of Success Mountain all by himself or herself. We reach it together!

"And that leads us to number three, which is that life is not always fair, so drive on! What does it mean to drive on? Life is going to mess you up on occasion. It is going to knock you down and rub your face in the dirt. As Dr. Robert H. Schuller said, 'Life's not fair, but God is good.' And with God on our side, who or what can stand against us? Answer: nothing and no one.

"That great philosopher Rocky Balboa said, 'It is not how hard you can hit. It is how hard you can get hit and keep moving forward.' In order to succeed in life, we have to realize that life isn't always fair, and we need to quit whining, suck it up, and drive on!

"Number four, failure can make you stronger. When a Navy SEAL hears the word 'circus,' they don't think of a big tent with three rings inside of it. They don't think of elephants, clowns, and lions being tamed. No, the Navy SEAL thinks of something very different when they hear the word 'circus.'

"In SEAL training, if you didn't measure up on an event on a given day, then you were put on the circus list. Maybe it was the obstacle course, and you were too slow going through the rope challenge. Maybe it was the distance swim, and you and your swim buddy came in last. For whatever reason, the instructors put you on the circus list.

"The circus list was an extra two hours at the end of the day of calisthenics and other strenuous exercises. Some of them were even done in water. By the end of the circus, you were exhausted. In fact, you were beyond exhausted. As you dragged your weary body to bed, you practically would fall asleep before your toes touched the inside of the blanket. Morning always came too soon after a circus, making the exhaustion you felt in the a.m. a predictor of another circus in the p.m. One failure seemed to build on another, with one circus after another.

"After a while, it began to dawn on you like the sunshine in your window that you were getting stronger. The circus was building your body. What started out as failure became strength.

"To complete SEAL training, each trainee had to pass a huge swim in the ocean. On that last big test, McRaven and his swim buddy pulled themselves up onto the shore to stare into the waiting eyes of their instructors. These instructors, who were all Vietnam vets, stared down at the raw trainees. Did they pass? No other swim duos were on the beach. Were they that far behind everyone else that they had already left the beach?

"One instructor looked at McRaven and his swim buddy and said something like 'Well done, SEALs. You are in first place.' Gesturing to the sea, the instructor continued, 'No other team is even in sight. Well done.'

"Don't be afraid of the circuses of life. No great achievement is accomplished without failure. If you never fail, then you aren't stretching yourself enough. Go for your dreams! Don't be afraid of the circus, because it can make you stronger.

"Next, number five—Admiral McRaven shared the motto of the British Special Air Services, the famous SAS. Their motto says, 'Who dares, wins.' Who dares, wins. You see, my friends, there is no success without risk.

"You will not reach the top of Success Mountain without adversity. The fear of that adversity is what keeps most people in the valley. What do you have down deep in your heart that is your greatest desire? Why have you given up on it? It is time to resurrect it and start the climb towards the peak. There will be tough times. There will be risk. But with great risk, there is the potential for great gain. Great gain not just for yourself, but for humanity.

"I know. I know. That sounds very grandiose. But where would humanity be if the Wright brothers chose not to dare to win on that beach at Kitty Hawk, North Carolina? Where would America be if George Washington and his colleagues hadn't dared to win in 1776? Where would humanity be if there were no America? Where would children's literature be if J.K. Rowling didn't dare to win? Where will we be if you choose not to dare to win?

"'Who dares, wins.' Choose today to dare to win, for your dreams reside on the other side of the rainbow.

"Number six is this: one person can inspire hope. The SEALs had to go through what they affectionately referred to as 'Hell Week.' Part of that week was spending hours up to your neck in the mudflats. Imagine your whole body covered with thick, cold mud. The only thing showing is your head. It was bone-chilling exhaustion, and the SEALs had to stay there all night until the sun rose over the horizon. If that wasn't bad enough, they had to endure hearing the constant bombardment of the instructors daring them to quit. The instructors would yell, 'If just one of you trainees quits, then the rest of you can get out of the cold mud. It only takes one, and the misery can stop. We have some nice hot soup up here for you. Come on! Just give up. You know you want to.'

"As the SEAL trainees were considering their fate, one small voice could be heard singing in the mud. The voice was off-key and would never make it on *America's Got Talent* reality show, but the voice was persistent. Soon, that one voice became two voices and then three. Soon, all the SEALs were singing in the mud.

"The instructors threatened them if they didn't stop singing, but the singing didn't stop. All of a sudden, the Admiral said the mud didn't seem as deep or as cold, and the dawn didn't seem so far away.

"It only takes one voice to inspire hope. It only takes one person to make a difference. You can be the next Mother Teresa, Dr. Martin Luther King, Jr., Billy Graham, or Abraham Lincoln. It only takes a little courage and a lot of gumption. And I see both of the qualities in spades here this morning."

The auditorium erupted with applause. Andrew smiled at his team. He then raised both hands into the air like a boxer who has won the Heavyweight Championship. One hand showed all five fingers outstretched. His other hand outstretched two fingers. He then said, "But—only if you have number seven. The last thing the Admiral told the students on that day in 2014 was to never, ever quit on their dreams.

"In the middle of the compound, there was a bell. All a SEAL trainee had to do to quit was to ring the bell three times. Ring it three times, and you could sleep in the next morning. Ring it three times, and you could rest your overworked, overexercised body. Ring it three times, and you could go home—as a failure.

"You may be sitting here this morning thinking, 'Andrew, that is pretty harsh calling them failures.' Understand that I am not calling a sailor a failure because he didn't make it as a SEAL. There are plenty of things in my life where I failed, but I gave it my best shot, and it just wasn't good enough. That doesn't make me a failure. Although, I will admit, there are sometimes in my life where I quit, and I hadn't given it my all. That is a different situation.

"Ringing the bells in life is quitting on your potential, and quitters never reach the top of Success Mountain. Almost always, quitters regret their decision to stop. Push on! As it is said, it is always darkest before the dawn. Push on! Give it your all, and if you don't make it to the top, then that is not failure. When you feel you can't go any farther, then look up—I dare say that, in most cases, you will find yourself closer to the mountaintop than you could ever have imagined. Push on!"

Andrew paused and looked over the audience. He raised his clasped hands to his lips as if in prayer, and then he said, "There you have it. Words to live by from an Admiral who has seen the darkest sunsets and the brightest sunrises. One, make your bed first thing every morning. Two, in order to win, you need to have a team. Three, life is not always fair, so drive on. Four, failure can make you stronger. Five, who dares, wins. Six, one person can inspire hope. And seven, never, ever quit on your dreams.

"You have what it takes, my friends. *We* have what it takes. Now, let's go get it done. Don't forget to grab a book on your way out of the auditorium. God bless you."

The auditorium erupted into a roar as the audience rose to their feet as if their team had just won the Super Bowl. As he walked off the stage, Andrew wiped away a small tear forming in his left eye. He truly was blessed with the best team. Andrew was beginning to believe they could actually become the number one children's book publisher in the industry.

CHAPTER 7: THE INFLUENTIAL LEADER ENLARGES PEOPLE

THE NEXT DAY Andrew got into his office early for his personal development study time. He sat down on the couch and placed his feet on the wooden coffee table in front of him. A smile formed as he thought of yesterday. It had been the best day. Not just the Weekly Motivational Summit, but everything about the day had been wonderful!

The building had been infused with tremendous energy. It was almost electric. Everyone seemed to be getting along better, working more productively, and having fun. Andrew said out loud to no one, or so he thought, "I enjoyed yesterday."

"And well you should," said a deep, gravelly voice behind him.

Andrew jerked around with a start. "Digger. You startled me. How did you get in? All the outside doors are locked this early. Of course, I don't mind you being here. I am just shocked."

"Oh, you know me. A locked door isn't so much of an obstacle as an opportunity. Hey, that is pretty good. I should write that down."

Andrew chuckled and shook his head. He then got up, walked across the office, and gave Digger a hug. "Come, sit down, my friend," said Andrew, gesturing to the couch.

After both Digger and Andrew had sat down, Andrew asked, "How did you know about yesterday? We haven't spoken for three days."

"Oh, I know lots of stuff… and I was in the back of the auditorium for your talk with your team. You are quite a speaker, Andrew."

Andrew waved his hand and said, "Nay. I was just passionate about the topic."

"Don't sell yourself short. Passion and enthusiasm are what it takes to be a great speaker and a great leader. A person can have all the leadership skills and still have trouble influencing people. On the other hand, a green, wet-behind-the-ears person can sway the world with their passion."

"I guess that makes sense," said Andrew.

"Let me put it this way: which leader would you rather follow—President Nixon or President Reagan?" asked Digger.

"No contest. Of course, Reagan."

"How about Steve Jobs or Steve Forbes?"

"Again, no contest," said Andrew. "Steve Jobs."

"All four of the men we just mentioned were, or are, in the case of Steve Forbes, very competent and, some might say, extraordinary at their jobs—but two were more influential. Reagan and Jobs had two special ingredients that the others did not. They had enthusiasm and the ability to sway an audience with the spoken word." Digger paused and then continued, "Anyway, what were you working on when I came in this morning?"

"I was just about to start my morning study session with the iPod you gave me."

"Well, don't let me stop you. Do you mind if I join you this morning?" asked Digger.

"No, not at all," said Andrew. That would be great." He turned on the iPod, and the two leaders began listening.

● ● ● ●

Once you know an individual's strengths, the next step is to enlarge them. Enlarging people is mentoring them. There are four steps to the successful enlarging process.

The first is to give them access to a training library. A training library includes personal development books, audio, video, and DVD programs. Encourage your team to become readers. Research shows that if we commit to reading one book a month in whatever area we choose to develop ourselves in, that in five years, we will be in the top five percent of experts in that area in the world. That is powerful, but it also shows how few people take action on this. So, what kind of time commitment are we talking about for the average reader to read one leadership book a month? About 15 to 30 minutes a day. That's it. A small discipline that can lead to your success. Amazon.com is a great resource for finding the books you want to read.

Research also shows the value of listening to audio programs. For example, I think it was the University of Southern California that discovered if we live in a metropolitan area, we could gain knowledge equivalent to a college associate degree in three short years just by listening to audio programs during our commute to and from work. Incredible! Audible (an Amazon company) is a great resource for audiobooks and audio programs.

The second step in enlarging people is to open them up to growing experiences. A growing experience can be just about anything. It can be serving on a committee, joining a project team, or attending a training seminar. Growing experiences not only help our team members improve; they help motivate them, too.

Step three is to challenge them to success. This means stretching your team member outside their comfort zone. In the fabulous little book *Running with the Giants*, John Maxwell expresses it this way, "Live in the faith zone, not the safe zone." Too many people are afraid of anything that makes them feel uncomfortable. But there is no growth without stretching. Just like an athlete who stretches before a competition, stretching outside our comfort zone prepares us for the future and greater success.

One caution: don't overstretch your team member. In other words, stretch them outside their comfort zone but not too far outside their comfort zone. Just as a baby doesn't go from crawling to running, your team member must walk before they run.

Step number four is to set them up to succeed. Remember, success breeds more success! Our job as leaders is to provide our team members with everything they need to succeed. If that is training, then give them training. If that is resources, then give them resources. If that is help and support, then give them help and support.

Believing in and enlarging your team members are prerequisites for your team's success. Do this, and you are virtually guaranteed success.

● ● ● ●

Andrew turned off the iPod and looked at Digger. Digger stayed silent, waiting for his young protégé to speak first. After a minute of silence that felt like an hour in a dentist chair, Andrew said, "That is good stuff, but it seems like it will take a long time."

"It can take a long time, but that doesn't mean it isn't worth it," said Digger. "Leadership and team development are more of a marathon than a sprint. Let me ask you a question. Did you and Laura get married after your first date?"

"Of course not. Who would do that?"

"Exactly," said Digger. The wise couple takes their time. They let the friendship grow like a caterpillar into a butterfly. Enlarging people is the same way. Growth takes time. Don't rush it. Just nudge it along its way."

CHAPTER 8: IT IS ALL ABOUT THE STROLL

"**I JUST DON'T** get it," said Dave Brittle. Dave was the Maintenance Manager at Steele Books, and he was having difficulty with his team. "I see how you are getting everyone excited and moving in the same direction. But Andrew, I can't get it to work with my team—and I only have three people on my team."

Andrew and his eight department heads met every Tuesday morning. The purpose was to discuss challenges like the one Dave was experiencing as well as update each other on projects within their departments.

Andrew leaned back in his chair and swiveled as he crossed his legs. Deep in thought, he finally lifted his head and looked around the conference table into the eyes of his leaders. He then settled on Dave. "Dave, I know it can be frustrating. Believe me, I know. I think you aren't getting out among the troops enough."

"I don't understand," said Dave. "What does it mean to get out among the troops?"

"As you all probably know, Lincoln is one of my favorite leaders to study," said Andrew. "He followed what we call today 'Leadership by Walking Around.' I doubt if that is what he called it, but he practiced it nonetheless.

"Lincoln believed that it was important to spend time with his team. To be seen by his team. In his case, this meant the Union Army troops predominantly. They were the ones who were going to win the Civil War. Lincoln went to the front lines often to either observe or even, in some cases, take charge of the battle situation himself. He was one of the few American presidents to come under fire while in office.

"As I mentioned a moment ago, this concept is called 'Leadership by Walking Around.' Dave, all you have to do is be present. Have an open door. Don't get sidestepped and stuck in the Ivory Tower, so to speak. Lincoln believed that getting out among the people was really the only way to know what was going on. As a lawyer, he was known for going out and discovering for himself what the real situation was. This is one of the elements that made him so successful as a lawyer and then later as President of the United States. Lincoln believed this so fervently that he relieved General John C. Fremont from his command. Lincoln said, 'His cardinal mistake is that he isolates himself, and allows nobody to see him; and by which he does not know what is going on in the very matter he is dealing with.'"

"Andrew, I see you leading by walking around all the time," said Chief Operating Officer Sally Benjamin. "Just the other day, I walked out onto the production floor and saw you with your sleeves rolled up and grease all over your hands. You were knee-deep helping with one of the presses. Lately, I have followed your example. I used to stay in my office and run operations from behind my computer screen, sending emails. Now, I make it a habit of going out on the floor three times a day."

Andrew smiled, and before he could respond, Dave spoke up. "Is it working for you, Sally?"

"Oh, absolutely," said Sally. "Dave, I know you are uncomfortable with this concept. You and I are made out of the same cloth. We are introverts, so anything that pushes us out in front makes us uncomfortable. But don't think of it as being *out front* as much as being *beside* your team. I have found it to be really successful. We catch problems before they turn into monsters. We have begun nipping them when they are just little annoyances. It is really pretty cool—and I am enjoying being out of my office and with my team."

Looking at Sally and then Andrew, Dave said, "OK. I will give it a try."

Vice President of Sales, Chuck Harrison, spoke up. "Dave, as your and my favorite philosopher —Yoda—said, 'Do or do not, there is no try.' Hey, you've got to bring a little Star Wars into every meeting."

"You always do," said Andrew with a chuckle. "Seriously, let's all spend a few more minutes each day with our individual team members. For me, that is all of you. You know my door is always open—and I will be walking around."

CHAPTER 9: THE MAN WHO KILLED 11 MILLION PEOPLE

"**VOTTO HITS A** hard line drive up the middle! The ball hits the second base bag and pops out into center field," said the Cincinnati Reds Hall of Fame announcer Marty Brennaman. "Votto is safe on first, and Hamilton scores. That puts the Reds up four to three."

"Oh, that was awesome," said Andrew. "Votto is still the best first baseman in the league."

"That he is," said Digger. "I haven't been to a Reds game since Jack Blake and I came a couple of years ago. I am glad you were free tonight. The drive to Cincinnati from Indy isn't too bad."

"I agree. The drive is pretty simple. Right down I-74, and before you know it, you are there. Your timing was perfect. I was going to be sitting at home by myself. Laura and the kids are down in Bloomington visiting her parents for a couple of days."

Two more innings passed with not much more than chitchat between mentor and mentee—and of course, a couple of hotdogs. Then, out of the blue, Digger said, "How do you kill 11 million people?"

"What?" asked a puzzled Andrew.

"*How Do You Kill 11 Million People?* It is the title of a thought-provoking little book by Andy Andrews. How could a leader have so much influence that he was able to kill 11 million people? In fact, that is a conservative number. He most likely killed many more than that."

"Who are you talking about?" asked Andrew, looking right at Digger now.

"Hitler, of course. How did he do it? I am not talking about what techniques he used to kill all those many people. I am talking about how he convinced people to go along with it."

"I d-d-don't know," stammered Andrew. "I love history, and I am fairly familiar with the World War II era, but I have never thought about that question."

"Well, you should. Now, I know that came out a little harsh, but it is a question that I have been pondering ever since I reread Andy Andrews's little book. You ought to read it too. Very enlightening."

"It sounds interesting. Isn't Andy Andrews that writer who writes all his personal development books in story form? Kind of like the late Og Mandino?"

"Yep! That's him. Andy is a friend of mine."

Laughing, Andrew said, "Somehow, that doesn't surprise me."

"Have you read any of Andy's books?" asked Digger.

"No, not yet. I have a couple of his on my list of books to read."

"Well," said Digger. "I would start with this one. It is written a little differently than his usual style. Not so much story—but all-engrossing and thought-provoking."

"That is an interesting way to put it. I have never heard it put that way."

"No other way to say it," said Digger. "It wakes up your mind and won't let you go until you deal with the questions it stirs."

"Hmm, I will put that book at the top of my list," said Andrew.

"Andy Andrews expresses something very interesting in the book. This isn't exactly verbatim, but he said that the past is what is real, and history is what somebody recorded that happened. You see, my young friend, they aren't always the same thing."

"What do you mean?" asked Andrew.

"We are taught from childhood to trust our history books and our history teachers. But do you think they are always worthy of that trust?" Digger stared intently at Andrew with those steel-blue eyes that burrow into the soul like a groundhog into the ground.

"Are you asking if they have their own agenda?"

Digger didn't say anything. He just let Andrew's question hover in the air. Andrew then said, "I think that some of them might have their own agenda. No, let me correct that. Some of them *do* have their own agenda. I had a high school history teacher who was definitely trying to sway us with his political beliefs."

"Do you think that is right?" asked Digger.

"I guess if it is in the right direction."

"So, you are saying that it is fine for a teacher to indoctrinate students as long as you agree with the indoctrination."

"No, I didn't say that," said Andrew, getting a little defensive. Digger raised up his left eyebrow as he continued to stare at Andrew. Andrew then said, "Well, I guess I *did* say that, didn't I?"

Softening the mood with a chuckle, Digger said, "Now, I am not saying it is right or wrong. I am just getting you to think about it. What happens if a history book is filled with a pack of lies, but we accept it as truth? We never even question it. A couple of generations down the road, and truth is gone. For example, there are whole generations of Americans who think George Washington cut down a cherry tree, and when he got caught, said to his father, 'I cannot tell a lie.' Did you know that was all made up? It never happened."

"I didn't know that."

"And that is the problem. If we don't know our past, then we will fall for anything. It was George Santayana who said, 'Those who cannot remember the past are condemned to repeat it.' And, I might add, that means we will repeat the good and the bad."

"A swing and a miss," said announcer Marty Brennaman. "Another Dodger goes down swinging. The Reds are on a roll tonight. After seven and a half innings, the Reds have six runs, and the Dodgers have four."

Digger and Andrew stood with the rest of the crowded stadium and sang "Take Me Out to the Ball Game" for the seventh-inning stretch. As they sat back down, Digger said, "So, how did the Nazis kill 11 million people? They lied to them."

"What do you mean, they lied to them? Who would fall for that?" Andrew realized he sounded a little judgmental. "I am not trying to sound judgmental. I am just having a challenge wrapping my head around all of this."

"Hitler told his inner circle how fortunate it was for them that people don't think. He said that people will believe a big lie even more than they will believe a small lie. So, what was the lie that killed eleven million people?

"The Nazi guards would come to a community and say something like this: 'The Russians are advancing. We don't have much time. Get your families together. We have trains coming any moment to take you to safety. Now, it is going to be very crowded on the trains, but it is for only a short time. We are going to take you to a place where you will be safe. Men, you will be able to work, and your families will be safe and secure. We even have schools ready for your children. Hurry now! The Russians are almost here.'"

Digger paused and clenched his jaw. He then continued, "And the people walked right up and boarded the trains. Many of the trains rode the rails right into the heart of the concentration camps. When the Jews entered those train cars and the doors were shut—it was all over. And what many people don't realize is that it wasn't just the Jews that the Nazis condemned to death. Anybody Hitler disagreed with found themselves in a concentration camp. Of the 11 million killed, about 5 million were non-Jews.

"And here is the point," said Digger. "As unpopular as it is to say, Hitler influenced a lot of people, and that made him an effective leader. And the bigger point is this— Hitler was evil, and he was a rotten leader and a monster. Andrew, great leaders are men and women of integrity. They seek the truth. They look beyond the history books and stare into the eyes of the past. And, by so doing, they find truth. And, as the Good Book says, 'The truth will set you free.'"

Andrew didn't hear or see much of the rest of the baseball game. He sat there pondering what Digger had just taught him. Digger sat quietly next to him, allowing the lesson to resonate in his mentee's mind and soul.

Andrew was finally awoken from his pondering when he heard the announcer excitedly exclaim, "And this one belongs to the Reds! Reds, nine, Dodgers, four."

CHAPTER 10: A PRACTICE OF INTEGRITY

IT WAS A warm night as Andrew and Digger exited Great American Ballpark with the herd of humanity in downtown Cincinnati. They made their way down Pete Rose Way and headed toward the Newport South-bank Bridge (affectionately known as "The Purple People Bridge"), which connects Pete Rose Way in Cincinnati to Third Street in Newport, Kentucky. The Purple People Bridge, a pedestrian-only walkway, is the longest of its kind in the United States that connects two neighboring states.

Andrew and Digger had parked in Newport before the game and now returned to Newport with thousands of happy Reds fans.

As they arrived at Digger's red convertible and were opening the doors, Digger looked at Andrew over the black canvas top which was now up and in place and said, "A friend of mine once said, 'Hold onto wisdom and integrity as if it were your very life—because it is!' That friend of mine is Mark Bowser. He is also an author."

After they had both gotten into the car, Digger reached toward the glove box and pulled out a crinkled newspaper column. "This is a column that Mark wrote recently. It kind of ties into what we have been talking about tonight—that leaders must be of strong moral aptitude. That the quality of the leader is more important than the effectiveness of the leader. Effectiveness without integrity leads to a Hitler. Integrity with Effectiveness helps us be more Christlike, and Jesus of Nazareth was the ultimate leader to model."

Digger handed the crumpled paper to Andrew and said, "As I wind my way out of this traffic, go ahead and read the article and let it soak into the midst of the swirling thoughts you are pondering already."

Andrew unfolded the newspaper article and began to read:

A PRACTICE OF INTEGRITY
BY MARK BOWSER

WHAT do you think: Should managers and supervisors teach right from wrong? Should a leader share their moral values with the people they lead? Before you are quick to answer those questions, let me remind you of all the companies that have fallen out of good standing because of unethical practices, companies that include WorldCom, Enron, and, unfortunately, so many others.

If we and our businesses are going to thrive, we must adopt into our lives and teach into other peoples' lives the attitude that character does mean something. It is interesting that this topic has become a national debate. This is good. Even though it doesn't appear that character wins all the time—TRUST ME; CHARACTER ALWAYS WINS IN THE END.

For the next few minutes, let me guide you on a journey to three values we must teach our teams and explore how we can motivate them to live those values.

The first value we must teach our teams is the value of **Integrity**. One motivational speaker used to define integrity as "wholeness." In his view, as long as you are whole or congruent to your values, then you have integrity. Well, he is half right. What if you have the value that it is fine to murder people if they have different beliefs than you? If you are whole and congruent to that value, then according to his definition, we can murder and still have integrity. That is why a half-truth can mess up your life. He is right that integrity is wholeness. But the dictionary doesn't stop there. It tells us exactly what to be whole to. It talks about adhering to honesty and morals, being whole to those values. That is the integrity we must live and teach.

The second value we need to impart to our teams is that of Leadership. Yes, true leadership is a value. So, what is leadership? Author J. Oswald Sanders defined leadership with one word—influence. Leaders are able to influence people to take action. I believe true leadership is "morality influence." We need to motivate people to put morality and ethical goals into action.

The third value we need to express is that **Means Matter**. The results-at-any-cost mindset is dangerous and wrong. It is what has gotten companies in such deep water. If we want to have true success, then we must be results-minded but with ethics leading the way.

All right, there you are, three values—Integrity, Leadership, and Means Matter. Now, how do you get your team to grab hold of them? I believe there are three ways to do that. One, you must live them. You set the tone. You are the example. You are the model. Two, teach them and preach them. You have to be the voice of right. President Theodore Roosevelt spoke of using his bully pulpit. You must use your bully pulpit to positively teach right from wrong. Third, expect them. Don't settle for anything less. Keep your standards high. Expect the best!

Leaders—I encourage you to not gloss over this short article cavalierly. Take to heart the three values and never stop teaching them, and by so doing, we can change the face of the marketplace and the world.

CHAPTER 11: IT'S ABOUT CONNECTION

IT TOOK ANDREW and Digger about 25 minutes to get out of the Cincinnati area and onto I-74 West, heading back to Indianapolis. They had driven another 20 minutes or so in relative silence except for K-Love playing on the radio. Digger pulled into the left lane and passed a white Honda Odyssey van filled to the brim with people. Digger thought to himself, "Another carload of happy Reds fans." The Reds attracted fans from Southern Ohio, Indiana, and Kentucky. He then glanced over at Andrew and said, "You got your iPod with you?"

"Always," said Andrew. "You never know when you will have a few minutes to listen—standing in a line, waiting for an appointment, or even driving in the car."

"Well then, let's listen to Jack Blake's Leadership seminar."

"Sounds good to me," said Andrew as he looked for a place to plug in the iPod into the dashboard. "Hey, where do you plug in on this old jalopy of yours?"

"Hey, watch it, my friend. This chariot is a classic."

"Uh-huh!" Andrew grunted.

Digger then reached into the glove compartment and pulled out a little square box. He then handed it to Andrew and said, "There you go."

Andrew rolled it around in his hands and looked it over. "What is this? Is it a speaker?"

"Oh yeah. It is the Dollar Sergeant Store's finest Bluetooth speaker under five dollars."

"Uh-huh," grunted Andrew again. "All right. How do you turn it on?"

"Oh, the little doohickey knob broke off the other day. Turn it over, and you see that slit there? That is where the knob was. You kind of have to ease your fingernail in that slit and slide over the 'on' mechanism."

Andrew gave Digger an *Are you serious?* look, poked his fingernail in the slit, and slid the speaker into the on position.

"You see, nothing to it," smiled Digger.

Andrew then linked up the iPod to the speaker and turned on the seminar.

● ● ● ●

Building connections with your team is arguably the most important thing a leader can do. If your team doesn't trust you—then it is over! Abraham Lincoln believed it was so important that he spent 75 percent of his time as President of the United States meeting with people. Lincoln believed that a leader must stay close to his people. And remember, his people included not just his staff and cabinet, but the legislators and the citizens too. There is many a story where Lincoln took the time to hear the concerns of a common citizen.

Now, security was a little different back then. If we lived back in Lincoln's day and wanted to bend the ear of the President, all we had to do was walk into the White House and sit outside his office door. And when he could, the President would fit us into his schedule if possible. Come to think of it, they may have been a little too lax with their security. If they had tightened it up, maybe one incompetent bodyguard on that fateful night at Ford's Theater wouldn't have been enough, and Booth would not have accomplished his terrible deed.

Anyway, leaders are others-oriented. Lincoln had a heart to help people. He also understood that people are a great source of information, a way of putting your ear to the heartbeat of the people. In other words, being others-oriented helps the leader understand the tone of the culture —what people are feeling and thinking. This is true, not just for the culture of a country, but also of a company, organization, or group.

There are four elements that I believe are important if a leader is going to build rapport. In fact, they are more action steps than simply elements.

Number One—Get Among the People. A number of years ago, Donald T. Phillips took it upon himself to write the first book ever written looking specifically at the leadership qualities of Abraham Lincoln. It is a landmark book that I recommend to all leaders. It is called *Lincoln on Leadership*. In the book, Phillips said, "Lincoln even went to the field to observe or take charge of several battle situations himself, coming under fire at least once (one of the few American presidents to do so while in office)."

In a nutshell, leaders need to be available to their team members. A leader cannot isolate himself all day from his team. You must be reachable by your team. You must be seen. Get out of the Ivory Tower and get on the field like Lincoln.

Andrew turned off the iPod and said, "I was just talking about this concept to my leadership staff the other day. I call it 'Leadership by Walking Around.' In fact, I have read that book Jack mentioned in the recording. I love learning about Lincoln, and Phillips's book about Lincoln's leadership is one of the best."

"I agree. Phillips's book is a landmark book. I gave Jack his copy of the book a few years ago. I was planning on giving you a copy too—but I hear you have already read it."

"Sorry, Digger. I didn't mean to burst your bubble."

"Not at all. It just means you are ahead of the game—and that is good."

Andrew switched the iPod back on.

● ● ● ●

Number Two—Get the Facts. As leaders, we don't have the luxury of not being in the know. We have to be up-to-date on all the fine details of what is going on. Now, don't misunderstand me. Getting all the facts doesn't mean you have to acquire those facts yourself, but that you have to be briefed on them. The President of the United States doesn't go out and collect the intelligence data, but he or she is briefed on the results on a regular basis.

Number Three—you need to have an open-door philosophy. So, what does this mean? It means you are approachable. Let me give you a couple of examples from people who have attended my business seminars. One gentleman told me that he makes one-on-one appointments with each and every one of his team members. This was their individual time with their leader. They could talk with him about anything. He made sure it was their agenda and not his. This is not a time for confronting or even correcting. It is a time for listening.

Another gentleman from my seminars had an equally effective approach but with a little twist. Instead of setting an appointment with each team member, he had open office hours. Kind of like a college professor. He told his team that he would be in his office at a certain time, and anyone who wanted to speak with him during that time could. He disciplined himself and made sure that he was in his office at the appointed times.

The greatest coach of all time, John Wooden, did something very similar for his basketball players. Coach Wooden set appointed times when he would be available for his team. A player could come and talk with Coach about anything—school, girls, basketball—anything.

Have an open-door policy and be approachable to your team. You will be amazed at what a little caring will do. As many famous leaders, including Teddy Roosevelt and John C. Maxwell, have said, "People don't care how much you know until they know how much you care."

Number Four—return favors before favors are due. Now, that is kind of an odd thing to say. So, what does this mean? It means one simple word—networking. We have to connect with people. One of the best books on this topic of networking was written by the envelope-manufacturing leader and mega-bestselling author Harvey Mackay. The book is titled *Dig Your Wells Before You're Thirsty*. The book is billed as the only networking book you will ever need, and it lives up to that billing. However, I do encourage you to read more than one book on how to connect and network with people. The late Charlie "Tremendous" Jones said, "You are today what you'll be five years from now, except for the people you meet and the books you read." So, read as many books as you can and on a variety of topics.

Let's go a little deeper in the meaning of returning favors before favors are due. I have worded this phrase in a very specific way. In order to return favors before they are due, you have to take action first. Many decades ago, a sales guru revealed to his audience the secret of selling and influence. He said, "Find a need and fill it." One of the greatest ambassadors of selling, Zig Ziglar, put it this way: "You can have everything in life that you want as long as you help enough other people get what they want."

That is what returning favors before they are due is all about. How can you help someone else? Where are you an asset in their life and business? Where can you make a difference? Answer these questions and take action on what you uncover and you are on your way to returning favors before favors are due.

• • • •

Andrew turned off the iPod. "That is an interesting concept. I have never heard it worded that way."

"It is a unique way of saying it," agreed Digger. "But don't lose the impact of the message in the oddness of the way it is worded. I will go so far as to say that the person who networks the most, and most successfully, I might add, will be the ultimate success. No matter what you want to accomplish in life, you need people. No one climbs Success Mountain by themselves. A writer isn't a success without an editor, possibly a literary agent, and most definitely a publisher. A salesperson isn't successful without the production and fulfillment side of the business..."

"...and I am not as successful without my mentor," added Andrew.

CHAPTER 12: THE MOUSE'S MESSENGER

THE FOLLOWING TUESDAY morning, promptly at 6:30, Digger picked up Andrew in front of Steele Books. The sun was beginning to poke its head over the trees. Andrew raised his left hand to shade his eyes. After Digger had stopped the car, Andrew got in. He had no idea where they were going that morning. Digger had simply said it was a surprise.

"So, where did you say we were going this morning?" asked Andrew, trying to trick Digger into giving away their destination.

"Ah, I didn't," said Digger. "However, that was a nice try, my young Padawan. Just a little Star Wars lingo to start out the day."

Not able to hold back a smile, Andrew joked, "All right, you old codger. Keep your secret. See if I care."

"Someday, you will be older than dirt, too," said Digger.

After a few minutes, they pulled off the highway onto an exit ramp that led right into downtown Indianapolis. "Traffic is light this morning," Andrew thought, "probably because we are up before the roosters." A few more minutes passed before Digger pulled into a parking garage next to the Convention Center and the Hyatt Regency. He found a parking space, and the two friends walked toward the elevator.

Digger then explained their destination. "What you are about to experience is what Napoleon Hill used to call a Mastermind Group. I am a member of three of them: one here in Indianapolis, one in Cincinnati, and one down in Orlando. A Mastermind Group is a small number of professionals who gather together frequently to brainstorm different challenges and opportunities that the different members are going through at the time. Each of my groups has about 10 to 12 members."

"It sounds interesting," said Andrew. "I have never heard of such a group."

"It is a powerful concept. More brains working together on a subject creates an energy of creativity that is hard to explain but always productive. Today, we have a special treat. A friend of mine from my Orlando group is up here on business. He is going to be our guest speaker today. You will love today's meeting. This man is a leadership genius. What he accomplished in his career is extraordinary at least and unmatched at best. I have to admit I am kind of excited myself."

They stepped off the parking garage elevator directly into a spacious, very contemporary-looking lobby. "Welcome to the Downtown Hyatt Regency," said Digger.

"I had forgotten how nice this place is," said Andrew. "Laura and I were here a few years ago for a wedding reception."

"At that visit, was the reception in The Eagle's Nest?" asked Digger.

"No, it was in the ballroom."

"Well, then you are in for a real treat. We hold our Mastermind meetings up on the roof."

"On the roof?" asked a puzzled Andrew.

"Well, almost," said Digger. "The Eagle's Nest is the revolving restaurant at the very top of the hotel. Literally on the roof. Best scenic views in town."

Digger and Andrew stepped off another elevator to enter a majestic round restaurant with windows all around. The restaurant moved so slowly that Andrew couldn't feel the motion as the eatery revolved around the cityscape.

Digger led Andrew to the far left of the restaurant, where a long table was set for a dozen people. At one end was a table-top lectern, which was obviously the head of the table. Digger walked right up to a distinguished-looking gentleman with salt-and-pepper hair. "Welcome, Lee. Glad you could make it. We appreciate you getting up early to join us this morning."

"Glad to be here, Digger. Anything for you, my friend. You have taught me so much over the years. I can't tell you how grateful I am. I have had many mentors over the years, and you were the best."

Andrew was a little puzzled. Digger and this gentleman seemed to be about the same age, but this man talked as if Digger had been the same wise guru many years ago that he was today. "Exactly how old is Digger Jones?" wondered Andrew to himself.

He was awakened from his reverie by a big hand slapping him on the shoulder and Digger saying, "Lee, I want you to meet a good friend of mine. This is Andrew Steele. He runs one of the best publishing houses of children's books in the entire world. Andrew, this is Lee Cockerell. Lee is the retired, yet inspired, Executive Vice President of Operations at Walt Disney World."

Andrew and Lee shook hands warmly and began chatting. They didn't even notice that Digger had slipped away.

A few minutes went by, and then Digger cleared his throat loudly. He was standing at the lectern at the end of the table. Digger then said, "Friends, welcome! The Eagle's Nest is about to serve our breakfast, and then we will have our meeting. Please take your seats."

Andrew and Lee discovered that their name tents were across from each other on the table right next to the lectern. Digger's name tent was on Andrew's right.

After they had eaten, Digger stood up and went to the lectern. "It is my great privilege to introduce to you our guest speaker. Lee Cockerell had a distinguished career at Hilton, Marriott, and Disney. He is the retired Executive Vice President of Operations at Walt Disney World Resort in Florida. At that position, Lee was in charge of operations at all the theme parks, water parks, hotels—everything. The entire kit and caboodle. He also led 40,000 cast members at Disney. He is the author of several books, including *Creating Magic*, which is one of the best leadership books in the last 20 years. He is here today to share his thoughts on how we can take our leadership influence to the next level. Please help me in welcoming Lee Cockerell."

As the Mastermind members applauded, Lee stood up and stepped to the lectern. He leaned in and whispered something in Digger's ear as they shook hands. Digger laughed and slapped him on the back. Lee stood behind the lectern, smiled, and began:

"Is it possible to create Disney-like magic in any industry? How about a small mom-and-pop bakery, or a factory making widgets and gizmos, or a car dealership—or how about your business? I am here to tell you a resounding 'yes' that you can create magic in your business, too.

"Today, we are going to talk about how you can transform your leadership and influence beyond what you thought was imaginable. So for the next few minutes, I am going to ask you to let me be your guide through what you might think is Fantasyland, but in reality, is your Tomorrowland. A Tomorrowland if you so choose it. You see, the dreamworld of Fantasyland will transform into Tomorrowland if you will do one thing— ACTION. Action is the key.

"This morning, I have six suggestions for you to take your leadership to the next level—to create magic in your life. Six suggestions, if acted upon, will take you to a land that Walt himself would be proud of. So, let's get right to it.

"Number one, be a storyteller. Storytelling is what Disney does best. But did you realize that storytelling is the greatest tool you can use as a leader? As I wrote in my book *Creating Magic*, 'Nothing better imparts more memorable lessons or inspires people to change their ways or spring into action than a tale well told.'

"Let that sink in for a minute," said Lee, looking over the small audience seated before him. "People remember stories more than just facts. People are inspired into action through stories. Lives are changed through stories. Abraham Lincoln was a master storyteller. If given a chance, he preferred to make his point in story because he knew that was what would have the desired impact—and that man literally saved a nation. And then there is the greatest storyteller of all—that carpenter from Nazareth that saved the world. So, what story will you tell? Stories are everywhere. Use them to influence your world.

"Number two, when giving feedback, don't just tell it, explain it. When my son Daniel was 16 years old, he got home a bit later than his mom, and I had instructed him to. In fact, it was well past midnight. His curfew was 11:30.

"Well, like any parent, I confronted him when he came in, and, of course, he owned up to his fault and politely said it would never happen again… and if you believe that, I really do have some swamp land for you to purchase back home in Florida. No, Daniel was a typical teenager. He got angry and accused me of setting an 11:30 curfew because that was the time I wanted to go to bed.

"I was at a crossroads. How do I respond? On this particular occasion, I kept my emotions in check, and I explained to him my reasoning instead of telling him 'because I said so.' I explained to Daniel I had read a report that said car accidents go up by 35 percent after midnight. That is because that is the time when most people leave the bars. I explained to Daniel that his mom and I had decided on the time of his curfew for his safety and not because we wanted to keep him from having fun with his friends. He still didn't like it—but he understood it and accepted it. That is the key. The next time you have a policy change or a key change in business practice to announce, try explaining it instead of telling it.

"That leads us to number three, which is to continually train your people. Disney is almost anal when it comes to training. Why do you think that is? Does Disney overdo it?" Lee paused and looked over the gathering of professionals. "We are just a small group here today. I really want to have a conversation. What do you think? Does Disney overdo it when it comes to training? Is training that important?"

Finally, a hand went up about halfway down on the left side of the long table. Lee gestured to the petite woman in her mid-50s with short brown hair, and she spoke. "Hi, Lee. I am Barbara Smith. I am the President at JMP Drilling."

"Hi Barbara," said Lee.

"I believe that training your team is the most important thing a leader can do for their organization and the people themselves," said Barbara. "Over at JMP, we make it a habit of training. And, I say the word 'habit' on purpose. We set training goals. My leadership team and I set training goals each year for the entire company.

We look at it from two lenses. One, what are we lacking? If there is something that we are missing or not doing well, then we have to improve it. Just like Disney, JMP doesn't settle for being less than our best, particularly if it directly impacts our customers. The second lens we look through is where can we be the best? And I mean the best in the industry. We look at our strengths and set goals on improving them. You can only be the best when it comes to a strength. You can only take a weakness to good or maybe great. But you can take a strength to extraordinary."

"Well said, Barbara. And I agree with you," said Lee. "You can never have too much training. The great Wizard of Westwood, John Wooden, won 10 NCAA basketball championships at UCLA in his last 12 years before retiring. The Bruins won seven in a row. Do you think Coach Wooden ever said, 'Well, we are good enough. We don't need to get any better.'? Of course not. Coach was adamant about improvement. He was adamant about success. But to Coach Wooden, it wasn't about winning championships or even games. It was about improvement and helping each of his players and the team itself be the best they could be. Coach said, 'Success is peace of mind, which is a direct result of self-satisfaction in knowing you made the effort to do your best to become the best that you are capable of becoming.'"

Lee paused and looked out again at the leaders before him. He then continued, "That is what training is about. That is why we focus on it so much at Disney, and that is why all of us should focus on it in our organizations.

"One more thought on this training topic. As the leader, we must lead the way for training at our organization. And by that, I mean that you need to train—to instruct—your people. Coach Wooden didn't leave all the instruction to his assistant coaches. Wooden was right out there with his team instructing them on the big items and the small items, such as his famous lesson on how to put on your shoes and socks properly in order to not get blisters. Here it is in a nutshell: great teachers usually make great leaders. Teach your team, train your team.

"Number four is something at Disney we call Stop/Start/Continue Discussions. This goes hand-in-hand with training. At Disney, I held regular meetings with different internal teams and departments to stimulate thinking toward processes, company policies, rules, and operating guidelines. We called them Stop/Start/Continue Discussion Meetings. We asked ourselves which processes we should stop doing, which processes we should start doing and which existing processes we should continue to do. It worked very well. We made sure we got rid of any outdated or ineffective processes, kept only the ones that were working, and created new ones to fill any gaps.

"Number five, be and stay passionate. If you don't love what you do, then you need to do something else. Looking back on my long career, I realize that the only times I actively looked for another position or company to work for was when I started to get bored. Or worse yet, I stopped believing in the company. But when I worked at Disney, this never happened. I was excited to get up—even as early as 5 a.m. Why? Because I knew I was going to be making magic all day long. And there is no better feeling than that. You gotta stay passionate!

"Number six is something we call the 'Seven Guest Service Guidelines.' I know we are short on time, and I have run a little long, so I will go through them quickly.

"To make the guidelines easy to remember, we have named each of them after one of the seven dwarfs in *Snow White and the Seven Dwarfs*. So, here we go. Guideline one is 'Happy: Make eye contact and smile!' We have all heard the saying, 'I didn't trust that guy. He wouldn't look me in the eye.' That is such a true statement. Look every customer right in the eye and give them a genuine smile of helpfulness.

"Guideline two is 'Be Like Sneezy: Greet and welcome each and every guest. Spread the spirit of hospitality; it's contagious!' Make people feel at home, and they will think of your business as a home.

"Guideline three is 'Don't be Bashful: Seek out guest contact!' If you are shy, then you need to push outside your comfort zone and get out there with the customers. Seek them out and find a way to help them.

"Guideline four is 'Be like Doc: Provide immediate service recovery.' If something goes wrong for your customer, then fix it immediately and make it better.

"Guideline five is 'Don't be Grumpy: Always display appropriate body language at all times!' Have you ever had one of those days when you just didn't feel like being at work? Of course. We all have. We have to make sure that our body language always speaks a sense of openness and friendliness towards the customer. Sometimes we just have to follow that old saying, 'Fake it till you make it.'

"Guideline six is 'Be like Sleepy: Create dreams and preserve the magical guest experience.' You gotta give your customers some 'WOW' experiences. Surprise them with an extraordinary customer experience.

"And last, but not least, number seven is 'Don't be Dopey: Thank each and every guest!' Didn't our moms always tell us to say please and thank you? Well, just listen to Mom.

"And those are the Seven Guest Service Guidelines that have made the Disney customer experience absolutely famous and the best in the world.

"So, in conclusion, if you want to create magic at your business, then one, be a storyteller. Two, when giving feedback, don't just tell it; explain it. Three, continually train your people. Great teachers usually make great leaders. Four, have Stop/Start/Continue Discussions. Five, be and stay passionate about your work. And six, live by Disney's Seven Guest Service Guidelines. And, my friends, if you do these six things, then magic is already in your life, and Tomorrowland is right around the corner. Thanks for having me today. God bless."

The audience applauded enthusiastically as Lee took one step back from the lectern. Digger jumped up with the agility of a 16-year-old, grabbed Lee's hand, and shook it with vigor. Without letting go, Digger stepped up to the lectern and said, "Let's give one more round of applause for Lee. He has surely taught us to create magic in our workplaces. I also have a surprise for you."

Reaching below the lectern, Digger pulled out a box about the size of a grapefruit carton and said, "I took the liberty of purchasing each and every one of you a copy of

Lee's book, *Creating Magic*." Turning to Lee, Digger said, "Would you be so kind as to stay a few more minutes and autograph these for us?"

"I would be delighted to," said Lee.

About 45 minutes later, Digger and Andrew were walking through the lobby toward the garage elevator. Andrew said, "Thank you, Digger. That was a great experience. I learned a lot—and got to meet Lee. Thank you."

"You are most welcome, Andrew. I knew you would enjoy it, and I knew that Lee could teach you a tremendous amount about how leaders create great experiences for their team members and their customers." Pointing a finger at the book in Andrew's hand, Digger said, "Don't just read Lee's book. Devour it and digest it. And above all, take action on it!"

"I will. I will," promised Andrew.

CHAPTER 13: FINDING GOOD PEOPLE IS A TOP PRIORITY FOR GREAT LEADERS

AS SOON AS Andrew opened the front door at Steele Books, he knew the motivation of the Mastermind Group breakfast was over as if it had been siphoned out of his spirit like gasoline out of a car by a crook. Something was going on.

He locked eyes with Deb Smith, who was manning her post at the front reception desk. She raised her eyebrows in frustration. "What is going on?" asked Andrew, glancing up the stairs towards the direction of the commotion.

"I am not sure," said Deb. "They have been at it for about 20 minutes. Something to do with new prospective employees."

"Well, so much for a nice morning. I guess this is why I get the big bucks," said Andrew, smiling weakly.

He walked up the stairs and found his Vice President of Sales, Chuck Harrison, Chief Operating Officer, Sally Benjamin, and Director of Human Resources, Doris McKinley, in a tug-of-war debate in the conference room. Andrew walked into the room and said, "Team, something got your skivvies in a bunch?"

Startled, the three of them grew deathly silent like a pumpkin after Halloween. Doris was the first to speak. "Oh, hi Andrew. We have a problem."

"Yes," said Sally, exasperated. "We need more people on the production floor. And none of the new candidates have been hired yet. Business is booming, and I need more people to produce the books."

Looking at Chuck, Andrew said to lighten the mood, "Here is the solution. Chuck, your team is obviously selling too much. Quit it! No more calling on book-stores!" The tight faces relaxed as Andrew continued. "Putting kidding aside, what is the challenge?"

"We need 4 new people to work the first shift, and I have interviewed 22 new candidates," said Doris. "Their resumés are almost identical when you compare experience and education. I just want to make sure I choose the right people. That is why it is taking so long."

"I appreciate your desire to be careful," said Andrew. "From experience, I know hiring the wrong person can be disastrous. But I think there is a balance we have to look at. Doris, you said the candidates' experience is almost identical. I am assuming you are talking about work experience. What about their life experience?"

At the same time, Doris and Sally asked, "Life experience?"

"Many times, life experience can show us more about the candidate than their work experience. Maybe their work experience is very little. But maybe they had to help raise their little brother and sister when they were 16 years old as they went to school and held down a job on the weekends. Maybe they excelled as a college athlete both in the classroom and on the field. You see, these things show more about who they are from a character standpoint—and that is much more important than anything you will see on a resumé."

Andrew paused and gestured toward the chairs around the conference table. He took a seat, and the others followed suit.

Andrew then continued, "Successful teams are made up of successful people. The late Jim Rohn, who was known as America's foremost business philosopher, said, 'Good people are found, not changed.' In the same seminar where I heard him say that, he also expressed that he had read a headline that said, 'We don't teach our people to be nice. We simply hire nice people.' Think about that for a moment. Isn't that a smarter approach?"

Andrew paused again and glanced upward as if in thought. "I remember one time when—I think I was still in college and just working here part-time—my Uncle Steve said to me out of the blue one day, 'You can't change people. People have to want to change. All you can do is show them the way and motivate them.' I have never forgotten that lesson. Being older and wiser, Uncle Steve knew I needed to hear it.

"Finding great people to join our team is a clever shortcut to our success," Andrew continued. "Here is what I want you to do. Doris and Sally, I want you to interview those candidates again—together. I believe it is important to have two people present during the interview process. I also believe it is important for a candidate to go through at least two interviews before we hire them. You see, they are all attempting to put their best foot forward during the interviews. That is natural and normal. Sometimes it takes a little time to find the real person. I also want you to change the questions you are asking them. Get them to talk about their personal lives—where they come from, challenges they have overcome, how they organize their time, and so on. Those are the questions that will reveal their character. All right? Does that sound good?"

"Yeah, that makes sense," said Doris.

"Thanks, Andrew," said Sally. "I guess we just needed a little perspective."

"I am glad I could help. Make this your top priority. Come back and tell me who you have hired within five days."

It only took three days for Doris and Sally to show up at Andrew's office, giddy as two schoolgirls getting ready for the junior prom. Andrew looked up from his desk and couldn't help but smile. "You two look like you just won the lottery." Kiddingly, he continued, "You are not here to give me your two weeks' notice, are you?"

"Not at all," said Sally. Looking at Doris, she said, "Do you want to give him the good news, or shall I?"

"Go ahead, you tell him," said Doris.

"OK. Well, we are thrilled to announce that we just hired four top-notch people to join our first-shift team. And I will add that they have great potential."

"From a resumé standpoint, you don't see potential," added Doris. "But when we looked deeper as you suggested and we began asking different questions, that is when we really began to see who they are. It was an exciting process."

"I think we should make this type of interview process a company-wide policy for all department heads," added Sally.

"You don't have to ask my permission," said Andrew. "You both are part of my leadership team. You are the Chief Operating Officer and the Director of HR. Make it happen!"

"We will," they said in unison.

CHAPTER 14: EMPOWERING TEAM MEMBERS TO BECOME LEADERS

THE NEXT DAY, Andrew and Digger were sitting in a red-and-black cushioned booth at a Steak 'n Shake diner in the Castleton area of Indianapolis. Digger took a slurp from the straw in his chocolate shake. Andrew inwardly grinned at how this giant of a man could be as simple as a child. He wondered if that was not only part of the mystique of Digger but also a secret of his success.

Digger looked up and said, "So?"

"What do you mean, 'so'?"

"Well, you obviously are pondering something. What is it, my boy?"

"Oh, it really is nothing," said Andrew. "I was listening to a national talk radio show on my way to meet you, and the host and his guest were talking about empowering teens. But they never really explained what empowering is and how actually to do it. I have just been mulling over what it means to empower someone and if it would work for my team."

"'Empowerment' has become a buzzword in our culture," said Digger. "And I believe that is a reason why that radio show you were listening to never explained what empowerment is and what it can accomplish when done properly. It is hard to define a buzzword because the lines get blurred. Empowerment, though, is a key ingredient for any leader if his or her team is going to be super-successful."

"How would you define it, Digger?"

"'Empowerment' means 'to give ability to.' To develop and train someone in the art and skill of doing something. But it is bigger than that. Let me give you an example.

"You see," continued Digger, "the problem with understanding empowerment is in how we give that empowerment to someone else. Let's take two of your team members at work. You have Chuck over there leading the sales team and Sally running the operations. So, you walk up to Chuck, and you say, 'Chuck, Project Sell More is now your baby. It is your program. Go get it done!' then you pause and say to Chuck, 'Oh, by the way, if you need to make any changes, then come and throw those changes by me first.' In this example, what do you think would happen to Chuck? How would he respond?"

"I guess he would feel kind of handcuffed. Like he wasn't really in charge of the project," answered Andrew.

"That is exactly right because that example is not empowerment. The challenge is that our culture thinks that is empowerment. Unfortunately, in many teams and organizations, that is how it is being implemented."

"Here is the challenge with the example with Chuck," continued Digger. "Chuck is given the responsibility for Project Sell More, but he isn't given the authority. True empowerment only exists when the team member is given both."

"Hmm. That makes sense," mulled Andrew.

"My boy, empowerment is an equation," said Digger. "The equation is not original with me, but one that I think explains the dilemma quite accurately." Digger scooted his silverware off his napkin and moved the papered cloth to the center of the table. He plucked a pen out of his shirt pocket and began to write. When he was done, he shoved the napkin over to Andrew's side of the table and said, "There you go. That explains it."

Andrew pulled the napkin closer. It read:

Empowerment = Authority + Responsibility

"Let's take Sally over in operations," explained Digger. "You say, 'Sally, Project Operations Right Way is your baby. You have authority and responsibility. You run it as you see fit. Our goal is XYZ. Go make it happen!' Now, Sally is empowered. It also continues to develop her leadership skills. And what do you think it does for you, Andrew?"

Andrew thought for a moment and then said, "Well, for one thing, it frees me up from having to be intimately involved in the project so I can work on some other things."

"Right," said Digger. "It makes the team and the organization stronger. There are some things that only you can do. It is your responsibility as President and CEO. So, you have to do those things. And there are other things which you are the most gifted at. So, it is wise for you to do those things too. You see how it works? Steele Books becomes a leadership-focused organization where all the people are freed to be their best and to do their best."

Andrew held the napkin in his hands and pondered, "What if I give all this responsibility and authority to Sally and she messes up?"

"Then you use it as a teachable moment," said Digger. "We all mess up from time to time. That is part of the process. Actually, learning from our mistakes is one of the most profound learning opportunities and can make us much stronger.

"Another point to remember," continued Digger, "is that you can't empower everyone the same way."

"What do you mean? Now I am confused."

"Well, let me ask you a couple of questions. Andrew, do you have the same strengths, experience, and gifts as Chuck? And does Chuck have the same strengths, experience, and gifts as Sally?"

"Of course not."

"Exactly," said Digger.

"Digger, I am not trying to be a pain, but that doesn't explain anything."

"Let me put it this way. Everyone has to grow at their own pace. If you over-empower someone with more responsibility and authority than they are ready for, then what happens?

"They would fail because they wouldn't be able to handle the pressure or situation," said Andrew.

"What would happen to them as an individual or as a leader?"

"I guess they would lose confidence," said Andrew.

"Right again. And so now, they would be in worse shape than if we had never empowered them. You see, when someone is over-empowered, they drown. And, unbeknownst to us, we are the ones holding their head under the water." Digger paused, took a breath, and said, "My boy, as you are learning, leadership has great rewards—and great responsibilities. Leaders are kind of like doctors. We have the motto 'Do no harm.' We are like a great coach who knows each of his players so well that he knows what situations they are more likely to shine in. And then the coach works with them in practice to stretch those situations. We want to stretch our team members, but not break them like an overstretched rubber band."

"That makes a lot of sense," said Andrew. But what about the opposite? Is it possible to under-empower someone?"

"What do you think?" asked Digger.

"I think so. If we don't give them enough responsibility and authority, then I think they would get bored. Maybe even a little stale at their job."

"That is right. That is why many people look for a new job. They need a new challenge, and they look for it outside the organization because they don't feel like it is available inside the organization," said Digger.

"How you implement an empowerment plan is as important as understanding what it is. I believe there are four qualifications that must be present before you can truly empower someone. Let's go through them," Digger continued.

"That sounds good," said Andrew.

"All right. The first qualification is position. Fred Smith said, 'Who can give permission for another to succeed? A person in authority. Others can encourage, but permission comes only from an authority figure: a parent, boss, or pastor.' Mr. Smith is right. If you aren't in a position of authority with the person you want to empower, then you can't empower them. You can motivate and inspire them but not empower them. You must have a position of authority to truly empower someone."

"That makes a lot of sense," said Andrew. "Otherwise, the person would think you are overbearing and overstepping. Kind of like a know-it-all."

"Some people call that a jerk," said Digger with the slightest smile on the corners of his mouth. Andrew nodded in agreement.

"The second qualification is relationship. You must have some sort of a relationship with the person you want to empower. If they have very little contact with you, then you won't be able to empower them effectively. Even if you are their boss, you can't empower someone unless you have a working relationship with them.

"Three, respect. There has to be mutual respect for the empowering relationship to be truly effective. It is a two-way street.

"The fourth qualification is commitment. As the leader, you are in it for the long haul. Remember, Andrew, you can't ever give a team member their assignment and then disappear to another project, never to be heard from again. As a leader, you need to be available—available for guidance, strength, and help. But this is also a two-way street. The team member must be committed to you as their leader and to Steele Books to do the very best job they can—committed to go the extra mile if necessary."

Digger paused, looking intently at Andrew. Convinced he was grasping the concept, he continued. "After those four qualifications are in place, you can then move to the empowering process. It also has four steps."

"The first step in the empowering process is to discover their strengths. How do you think you do that?"

Andrew thought for a minute and then said, "Well, you could go back and look at what they have succeeded at in the past." Andrew paused, waiting for Digger to say something. Digger said nothing, so Andrew concluded that he wanted him to say more. "And you could observe them at their current job to see what they are good at."

"You are right on both counts," said Digger. "If you are naturally good at something, that is a clue of an inborn strength. But realize that most things are also teachable. All skills can be learned. Now, that doesn't mean that everyone is suited for all skills. If someone hates math, then I don't want them as my CPA. Because even though they can learn the skills of accounting, they would probably be sloppy at best or downright lousy as an accountant. Does that make sense?"

"It sure does," said Andrew. "People are usually better at something they enjoy doing."

"You got that right. The second part of the empowering process is to help them **develop their strengths.** This is where you become a coach. In my opinion, the greatest example of this was the late John Wooden. Coach Wooden led his UCLA Bruin basketball team to a record 10 NCAA championships. They won those 10 national championships in 12 years—7 of them in a row. Absolutely mind-boggling!

"Now, here is the key, Andrew. Coach Wooden didn't talk to his team about winning. He talked with them about improving and being the best they could be, both individually and as a team. Listen to how he defined success: 'Success is peace of mind, which is a direct result of self-satisfaction in knowing you made an effort to do your best to become the best that you are capable of becoming.' That is a great coach."

"I remember my Uncle Steve talking about watching Coach Wooden's teams play in those championships," said Andrew.

"It was a sight to behold. Kind of like poetry in motion. Think of your team members' strengths like muscles. Without use, muscles will atrophy. With continued use, they will grow. Stretch them like raising the weight of an exercise dumbbell, and they will grow even more. Powerful stuff. This is my favorite part of the process."

"So, what is the next step after helping them develop their strengths?" asked Andrew.

"The third step in the empowering process is to give them a place to use their influence. Let me explain it this way. One of Coach Wooden's great players was center Bill Walton. Bill Walton was loaded with talent, and Coach Wooden helped develop those strengths. But what if Coach never put Walton in the game? Those talents and strength would go to waste. You see, we must put our team members in the game.

"And that leads us directly into the fourth step, which is to help them succeed. As good of a basketball player as Bill Walton was, he still wasn't perfect. He made mistakes like everyone else. When our team member makes a mistake or gets off track, then we coach them back on target. Sometimes it is a strategy change that needs to be adjusted, and sometimes it is a technique. Everyone needs a coach. A coach can pull out the best in a team member."

Andrew thought for a minute, took a sip from his milkshake, and said, "You know Digger, I can see this changing Steele Books tremendously. Not only will empowering others free me up to work on the things that only I can do, I see it giving us a leadership-weighted organization—in a good way."

"It definitely is in a good way," responded Digger. All effective organizations are led by a leader at the top and then leaders all the way down the ladder, so to speak. Remember what John Maxwell said, 'Everything rises and falls on leadership.' Andrew, I suggest you choose three people on your team and make a list of ways you can empower them. Then, commit yourself that within the next week, you will start the process."

"You got it, Digger! I will make my list and plans as soon as I get back in the office."

CHAPTER 15: GRACEFUL LEADERSHIP

THE FOLLOWING DAY, Andrew was eating in the company cafeteria with an assortment of his team members. He had been making a habit of doing this about twice a week for the last month and discovered he was building deeper relationships with many of his team members. They were sitting at a round table on the right side of the cafeteria. The table looked out into the courtyard that was sandwiched between the office wing and the printing floor of the company. Many people were sitting at the multitude of umbrellaed picnic tables that were sprinkled on a large patio in the courtyard.

Just as Andrew took a bite of his ham and cheese sandwich, Kasey Smithson from the graphic design department said, "Andrew, we are really enjoying spending time with you during lunch. Thanks for doing so. I have never had a boss willing to eat lunch with us and talk with us like we are equals."

Swallowing his bite of sandwich, Andrew said, "Kasey, we are all equals here. We are equal in the eyes of God, and so we are equal here at Steele Books. We all just have different jobs and different responsibilities. But we are still equal."

"Hey Andrew," said Pete Rath, the first-shift pressman for Press Two.

"Yes, Pete."

"I am just curious… I love to read, and I am looking for a new book to digest. What do you read?"

"Ahh, I love that question," said Andrew. "I just finished a great book titled *Dream It! Do it!* It is written by famed Disney Imagineer Marty Sklar. Marty started with Walt Disney himself right before Disneyland opened. Sitting here in the cafeteria kind of reminds me of a story that he told in the book.

"Before I tell you the story, let me back up for a minute. I believe that we are all leaders and the first person we lead is ourselves. Then, we expand our leadership outward with our influence. The story I am about to tell you, I believe, is a perfect example of what I call 'Graceful Leadership.' Walt Disney could be a hard-driving, blunt man. But he was also a compassionate man who would sacrifice anything for his team. As the story goes, one day, Walt walked out of the Disney Studio Animation building into the bright California sunshine. As was his habit, as well as the culture in those days, Walt pulled out his lighter to light his cigarette only to find that the lighter was defective and wouldn't ignite.

"Seeing Walt's predicament, Ken Anderson promptly came to his boss's rescue. Ken was one of Disney's great story and character geniuses on the animation team. As he lit Walt's cigarette with his own lighter, his lighter became too ambitious, and Walt's mustache caught on fire. If that wasn't bad enough, a large portion of the animation staff had witnessed the fiery debacle.

"Well, of course, they got the fire out very quickly. As you can imagine, though, Ken didn't sleep very well that night. He tossed and turned and could only imagine the worst. The next day around noon, Ken's nightmare became reality when he was summoned to Walt's office.

"Ken knew his days were about to end at the Disney Studios. In his mind, he went through his resumé, thinking of whom he could get a job with after Walt fired him. When Ken arrived at Walt's office, the legendary studio head was waiting for him. Walt said to Ken with a bright smile on his face, 'Come on, Ken—let's go eat lunch.' Walt then led Ken to the Disney cafeteria where they enjoyed lunch together.

"Now, that is graceful leadership in action. By that time, Ken's unfortunate episode of the day before had already spread like wildfire around the studio. You know how it is around here. News travels fast. The same thing happened at the Disney Studios. Everyone knew about it. Walt understood this. Taking Ken out to lunch at a restaurant would have been nice—but taking him to lunch in the Disney cafeteria where everyone could see them and experience the forgiveness for themselves was priceless.

"Walt put back together Ken's credibility with the animation staff. It also lifted up Walt's leadership, too. People knew that Walt could be demanding. That he expected quality and their absolute best. But they also knew they were loved and didn't have to be perfect."

Andrew bent his head in thought. He then looked at his team members around him and said, "Now, that story is not why I started having lunch with you. But it is a lesson to me to always do my best to show grace and love in the midst of our busy, hectic business." Then, looking right at Pete, Andrew said, "That is one of the best books I have read in a long time. I highly recommend it. I think you would enjoy it."

CHAPTER 16: THE LEADER'S TOOL CHEST OF CREDIBILITY

THE NEXT MORNING, Andrew stepped out of bed and pulled back the window curtain in the master bedroom to see what the day looked like. To his surprise, there was a crisp coating of new white snow.

"Hey honey," he called to Laura, who was already up and getting dressed in the bathroom. "There is snow out there. It looks like about three or four inches. I didn't know we were supposed to get snow."

"Well, that is because you fell asleep right after the Indiana - Purdue game and missed the weather report on the local news. They said we might get another two or three inches throughout the day, too."

"Wow, I had better get going. Traffic is going to be a bear."

"The shower is yours," said Laura. "I will go down and fix breakfast before I need to get the kids up. How about oatmeal?"

"It sounds great. Thanks, honey. I will be down in about 15 minutes."

Andrew was right. Traffic was awful that morning. I-69 was bumper-to-bumper. "It is a good thing I have my iPod with me. It looks like I am going to be here a while," thought Andrew. He made a quick call to the office to let them know he was running late, and then he turned on the iPod. Immediately, that rich voice of Jack Blake came on:

• • • •

In order to be successful, a leader must have credibility. In fact, unless you have credibility in the eyes of your team members, they won't follow you. So, in this section, we are going to discuss the four tools in the Leader's Tool Chest of Credibility. I want you to think about your tool chest at your house. Go out to the garage or wherever you keep it. Open it up. What do you see? I can almost guarantee that you will see at least two tools. Can you name them?

That's right. A hammer and a screwdriver. In my opinion, you don't have a tool chest unless you at least have a hammer and a screwdriver. These are the basics and some of the most important tools. Just like your tool chest, a leader must have a hammer and a screwdriver. These basic tools together make up the first tool in our tool chest of credibility, and it is called Lead by Example.

A number of years ago, I worked on the production staff of SGW International. They are the organization that puts on the large Right Way seminars. They are some of the largest business seminars in the world. One of my main responsibilities was to sell the resource products for the events, such as books, videos, and audio programs. I remember a very busy seminar. I think we were in Denver. We had a lot of people wanting to invest in the resources—so many that we had too many customers. Now, that is a good thing, but it is still a challenge to service them effectively.

During the seminar, SGW's number two guy came up to me and asked, "Jack, how can I help?" I said, "I need people." What I meant was that I needed him to transfer some people from the other teams to my team for the short term. What he did was even more impressive. He jumped behind the table and started serving customers himself. He figuratively rolled up his sleeves and jumped on the front lines with his team. That made an impact on me. He showed me that day that he wasn't going to ask me to do anything he wasn't willing to do himself. He led by example. That day, his credibility went way up in my eyes.

The second tool in our toolbox of credibility is the power saw, and it represents communication. I think many times, we as leaders use our words too casually. Words mean something. Communication can be one of our greatest dreams come true or our worst nightmare.

Has anything like this ever happened at your office? A team member asks, "Can I have Friday off? I need to take care of (blank)."

You say, "Sure, not a problem."

Thursday rolls around, and the circumstances have changed, so you go up to your team member and say, "Sorry, you can't have Friday off now."

By doing this, what have you taught your team member about you and your word? That you can't be trusted. Now, I understand that sometimes circumstances do change, but all I am really saying is to be careful how you use your words. There is nothing casual about effective communication. Relaxed, yes. Casual, no. Words mean something, and we have to do our best to always be truthful, accurate, kind, courteous, and clear.

The third tool is the tape measure. You'll use it to communicate the vision and mission statements of your organization. Why does your organization exist? Where are you going? How do you plan on getting there? Not always easy questions. But they are some of the most important questions that you can answer for your team. Those answers will make a world of difference not only in your leadership credibility but also in your results.

The fourth and last tool is the glue. It will remind you that before you delegate, do some of the ugly tasks yourself. If all you do is delegate the ugly stuff to your team and keep the nice, clean tasks for yourself, your credibility will drop like a muddy brick in a pond. My best advice is to do some of the ugly tasks yourself. Delegate some of the clean tasks. Why? Well, your credibility will go up in the eyes of your team. You see, the time will come when you will need more help, and then when you delegate those ugly tasks, your team will jump in and pick up the ball. Why? Because they know it isn't that you are unwilling to do the ugly tasks; it is that the team is in crunch time, and you need their help.

Well, there you have it. Four tools to greater credibility. One, the hammer/screwdriver; two, the power saw; three, the tape measure; and four, the glue. Use these four tools regularly, and before you know it, your team will trust you, believe in you, and follow you.

• • • •

Andrew pulled into the parking spot at Steele Books and turned off the podcast. He said out loud to himself, "It is time to build more credibility."

CONCLUSION: ONE SMALL STEP... ONE GIANT HORIZON

THE NIGHT BEFORE, Digger had texted Andrew and asked him to meet him at Monument Circle. As Andrew walked up the familiar steps, he saw Digger waving to him from the top railing.

"Top of the morning to you, my boy," said Digger.

"Hey Dig, how's it going?"

"With a sunny morning like this, it can't be bad. Of course, every morning is sunny on the inside."

Andrew shook his head and grinned at his mentor. He then said, "What's up? You were pretty persistent about meeting this morning."

"Well, my boy, it is time for you to fly and for me to say goodbye."

"Goodbye! What do you mean, goodbye? Where are you going?"

"Andrew, you are more than ready to fly without a safety net. I am so proud of you. You don't need me anymore. You are becoming the leader God meant you to be. And there are many other people who are waiting for their mentor to appear. So, I must go. Remember this, though, as Dr. Robert H. Schuller said: 'Trust in God, believe in yourself, dare to dream.' You will go far, Andrew Steele. The world is your canvas."

With that, Digger gave Andrew a bear hug and slapped him on the shoulder. As Digger began walking down the stairs, Andrew could almost see a shimmer around him as the sun poked out of the clouds. As Andrew watched him go, Digger's image began to fade into the sunlight. Before long, he was gone, and Andrew was alone at the railing.

"Who is Digger Jones?" asked Andrew out loud.

A man about eight feet away looked toward him and said, "Excuse me?"

"Oh, nothing," said Andrew. "You wouldn't believe me if I told you. Have a good day." Andrew walked down the stairs and into a future which he knew was very bright indeed.

ABOUT THE AUTHOR

WHAT HE DOES: Mark teaches people and organizations how to win in leadership, selling, and customer service. Do you want to grow your sales? Maybe it is more appropriate to say that you *must* close more sales—and that you must close them now! Or maybe you have a revolving door at your business entrance. Sure, customers are coming in—but then they leave, to never be seen again. You need repeat customers. Customers who are loyal. So, whether you want to improve your results in closing more sales or create loyal customers who sing your praises—Mark Bowser can help you do that!

HIS BACKGROUND: Mark has been a professional business speaker since 1993. He has had the honor of presenting thousands of seminars and keynotes to help organizations and individuals reach peak performance.

ORGANIZATIONS MARK HAS TRAINED INCLUDE:

Southwest Airlines

Princeton University

Purdue University

Ford Motor Company

Delta Faucet

Anderson University

Physicians Surgical Care

Sony Music

United States Air Force

Kutztown University

Herkimer County Community College

St. Luke's Methodist Church

FedEx Logistics

Dallas Public Schools

Kings Daughters Medical Center

United States Marine Corp

Office of the Inspector General, DOD

"I must say I've attended many seminars and workshops, and by far, this was the best. Mark was inspiring, knowledgeable, funny, and just a wonderful speaker. He held our attention for two days, and then we wanted to hear more."

Charlene Cooke, Rutgers University Health Service

Over the years, Mark Bowser has proven his leadership skills time and again. However, it is not his skills that cause people to want to follow him; it is his character. Bowser is a man of old-fashioned character and integrity. Whether it is the businesses he and his family own, his political leadership, or leadership at church and community, Bowser is making a positive impact.

Mark Bowser is a polished storyteller and author of several books, including *Sales Success* with Zig Ziglar, *Some Gave It All* with Danny Lane, which is endorsed by Chuck Norris, *Nehemiah on Leadership*, and *Jesus, Take the Wheel*. He is one of the top professional speakers in the United States, having successfully trained many organizations, including Southwest Airlines, Dell, Ford Motor Company, United States Marine Corp, FedEx Logistics, and many more. He is the host of the popular podcast *Let Me Tell You a Story with Mark Bowser.*

Bowser lives in the Cincinnati area with his wife and three children.

NEXT STEPS: If you would like to check Mark Bowser's speaking availability for your next event, then please send him an email at mark@MarkBowser.com. We also invite you to visit www.MarkBowser.com and register for our free newsletters so that you can receive product discounts and updates on Mark's upcoming books, as well as discover how you can sell more, serve customers passionately... and create customer loyalty.

MORE BOOKS BY MARK BOWSER

Check them out at www.MarkBowser.com or www.Amazon.com/author/markbowser.

Sales Success by Mark Bowser (Contributions by Zig Ziglar, Tom Hopkins, and Scott McKain)

"Great Read! First of all, you can't argue with the 'A-list' contributing to this book. It reads well, is laid out nicely, and is easy to pick back up on during my hectic schedule interruptions. As a dentist, I am not a 'salesperson' and I do not force or try to talk patients into treatment. However, creating trust and value for a product or service correlates to ANY profession. Learning how to create that value, present the issue/items, and communicate is key.

Some patients want ideal health, some want beauty, some want it all. Some are realistic and some aren't. Unfortunately, a lot of healthcare workers cannot communicate findings, benefits or risks from treatment, or negatives from forgoing treatment well. As a result, there are a lot of untreated patients out there.

As healthcare workers, it is good to hear feedback and views 'from the outside' (like a patient ourselves) so we know how to better our game, not talk over our fantastic patients, and in the end, better our patients! This book helped me see views from a patient (i.e., non-dentist) perspective and the coaching from this rock-star team of contributors is spot-on.

I highly recommend this book by Mark Bowser. Thanks for a great read!"

—Jane Kirkpatrick

"I have been in sales for 20 years so, as you can imagine, I have read a lot of sales books. This book was by far my favorite! I normally approach a sales book as required reading but I found myself looking forward to each chapter!

Mr. Bowser expertly weaves great sales tips and best practices into a fictional story about a salesperson who, in the beginning of the book, is down on his luck and struggling with his sales. As the story progresses, the main character learns a better way to be successful.

I would recommend this book to all sales professionals and to non-sales people who enjoy a great story!"

—Pamela

Some Gave It All by Mark Bowser and Danny Lane

"Danny Lane and Mark Bowser have written an exciting roller coaster of an adventure. The amazing thing is that it is a true story. *Some Gave It All* grabbed me from the first paragraph and wouldn't let go until the last."

—**Pat Williams,** Orlando Magic Senior Vice President, author of *THE SUCCESS INTERSECTION*

"*Some Gave It All* shows the horror of war and the emotional toll and recovery of a real American hero, Danny Lane. Without brave Marines like Danny Lane, we would not be free. After reading this book, I will never forget that."

—**Lee Cockerell,** Executive Vice President (Retired and Inspired), Walt Disney World®Resort and Best-selling Author of *Creating Magic, The Customer Rule, Time Management Magic,* and *Career Magic*

"This is an amazing story of courage and sacrifice. I'm almost at a loss for words. Every God-fearing American ought to read this. It'll get your heart pounding and you'll be forever grateful for the men and women who keep this country safe, including American hero Danny Lane. I am proud to have him on my staff as a combat tactics instructor."

—**Jason Hanson,** Former CIA Officer, Author of the *New York Times* Best Seller, *Spy Secrets that can Save Your Life*

Bible in A Year (Mark Bowser wrote the monthly devotions)

Nehemiah on Leadership

Three Pillars of Success

To get a Mark Bowser autographed copy of *Some Gave It All*, please go to www.MarkBowser.com/SomeGaveItAll-Book